Point of Power

Kay Snow-Davis is a founder and board member of the Global Family Education Center on the island of Kauai, Hawaii and is on the board of directors for the Rocky Mountain Spiritual Emergence Network. She lectures internationally to management and employee groups and also maintains private healing practices in Boulder, Colorado and Los Angeles, California. Her latest project, as president of the Star Child Corporation, is the establishment of an "International Community Prototype" on Kauai, to be ecologically in tune with the earth.

POINT OF POWER

A RELATIONSHIP
WITH YOUR SOUL

Kay Snow-Davis

ELEMENT
Rockport, Massachusetts ● Shaftesbury, Dorset
Brisbane, Queensland

First published in the USA in 1995 by
Element, Inc.
42 Broadway, Rockport, MA 01966

Published in Great Britain in 1995 by
Element Books Ltd
Shaftesbury, Dorset

Published in Australia in 1995 by
Element Books Ltd
for Jacaranda Wiley Ltd
33 Park Road, Milton, Brisbane, 4064

Cover design by Max Fairbrother
Typeset by Create Publishing Services Ltd
Printed and bound in the USA by Edwards Bros. Inc.

British Library Cataloguing in Publication
data available

Library of Congress Cataloging in Publication
data available

ISBN 1-85230-633-5

DEDICATION

This book is dedicated to my children
all of you

You taught me to trust myself enough
to truly discover who I am
and live my point of power

Mahalo nui loa for being who you are
and being in my life

Contents

Foreword

E very epoch, culture, civilization and spiritual movement throughout the millennia of human consciousness has formulated the notion of the magical Tree of Life.

This Tree of Life has been represented in painting, song and myth, passed from generation to generation as a cornerstone of human interaction with earth, air and cosmos. It represented a connectedness, both literal (physical) and spiritual (metaphysical) between human beings and their total environment, across time and in space while still being grounded in everyday living.

With the onset of modern science and the industrial revolution, much of this ancient awareness was buried amidst the infatuation with mechanization, uniformity, productivity and progress and the resulting dissociation of human beings from the life source.

Over the past decades, while some technical progress has been achieved, a malaise of spirit has arisen that threatens not only human relations but the health and well-being of the planet.

Point of Power illuminates the Tree of Life wisdom of the ancients and reconnects it in a new way, suitable for the modern age of high technology and information overload.

This book illustrates a new approach to understanding yourself and your spouse, parents, children, co-workers and leaders. It supplies practical guidelines, examples and exercises.

As author, teacher and practitioner, Kay Snow-Davis gives us a great gift of spirit and practicality, enjoyable reading, with humor and compassion for all. She brings Tree of Life wisdom forward, into the present, and weaves it into words that allow us to reconnect ourselves, to heal our spirit, to transform our everyday being and progress toward fulfilling our individual journey.

Christina Crawford, Chesapeake Bay, Maryland
Author, *Mommie Dearest*
and *No Place to Hide*

Introduction

E = MC² = LOVE

It was 4 A.M., on a hot July night in 1984, at Two Bunch Palms, California. I sat straight up in bed in a very dark room and saw the beloved face of Albert Einstein, a bright, shiny, joyous face, as big as the whole room. He said, "E=MC² = LOVE. This is what the fourth dimension is; it is the frequency of Love, and it is available to all of you now."

I saw the formula, E=MC², to the right of Einstein's face, written in neon lights as though on an invisible blackboard.

This was the first time I had ever awakened like this and had a famous "visitor." Needless to say, I was awake the rest of the night! This was an experience for me, not just a vision. I felt the Love in my body and I saw the magnitude of this information. I was shown my past life, as though it were a movie and how this principle of Love has always applied in my personal life. Then I was shown how it applies on the planet.

This principle of Love sustains the Divine Order on Earth, for all life. It truly guides our souls as human beings, from the place of creation, regardless of how we think. Just as our bodies breathe, whether we are conscious of our breath or not, Love guides and renews our bodies and this Home Planet, regardless of our belief systems.

Point of Power is a place of expression for our souls, and one of the ways we deliver love throughout our life. Just as we may not be aware how the fourth dimensional energy of Love influences our daily lives, we may not be consciously aware of our Point of Power, and who we *really* are.

This book shows how to claim your "Point of Power" and remember your uniqueness, your naturalness and your magnificence. You are powerful now. You always have been powerful and you always will be powerful. That is your Divine Heritage, your naturalness. When will you choose to remember who you are, and release your power and naturalness?

Life is an adventure story and you are the author. Give yourself permission to consciously rewrite your life story now, view it from a fresh perspective. You influence the events in your life by the choices you make. The amazing thing about acquiring new understanding is that it allows time for a deep breath, a step aside, and a look at life with new awareness, appreciation and new options. Every choice you make that creates change in your life is like a rung on a ladder. Each step supports the expansion of your reality. That expanded reality gives more options and choices in relationships with our bodies, with each other and with the Earth.

The human mind is a phenomenal gift—a true partner with your Point of Power in creating fertile ground for receptivity. What beliefs fill your head? Do they work for you? Do you like the way you think about yourself and others? Do you like the way your life is working?

You can change if you want to. You have choices in what to believe and experience in life. If it doesn't feel good, change it. Be aware of what you're feeling and recognize the signals that changes are needed.

Long ago, you had a Divine relationship with yourself, an intimate relationship where you knew your Truth, felt Home in your heart, and lived the Law of Love with all your relations. This book is about going Home again, *accepting* yourself and others, and *allowing* Love to guide your life.

Your Point of Power is a sound from your Divine Essence, your Eternal Soul, the magic Child Within, your Naturalness, your Magnificence, your Excellence. It is your Point of Creativity, motivated by Love not Fear.

As you remember, and reclaim, your Point of Power, your outer world will begin to shift. It may not change in appearance, but in your attitude toward your life—your relationships and you.

Your requirements on this journey of remembering who you are include:

1. Give yourself a break.

2. Discover, rather than judge, yourself and your uniqueness.

3. Plug into your Point of Power, your strength, to express your naturalness, joy and beauty and notice how you feel when that happens.

4. *Take the lid off.*—Let unworkable beliefs find a way to eject from your mind, your creative laboratory.

5. HAVE FUN.

Chapter 1

Divine Instrument of Sound

We are like broadcasting stations, receiving energy from the universe and transmitting our bodies' natural rhythms through our minds and hearts. Our particular broadcast frequency is a soul level choice. We're born carrying the true sound for our path of life. Our joy in life is released as we hear this Truth, and "sing our song."

Through life's conditioning and experiences, most of us create beliefs and behaviors that lessen the expression of creative rhythm. These beliefs and behaviors are in opposition to free-moving energy, joy and wellness, forcing our lives to function through stress and distortion of our Points of Power.

Point of Power is where the Child/Soul within us is free—to speak, sing our song, create, play, and to love and be loved naturally and easily, without distortion or stress.

To reduce stress, we need to change the beliefs and behaviors that distort our Points of Power, begin remembering who we are, and transmit our natural rhythm.

I'm aware of four rhythms we can access, and each of them is an active creator. Your Point of Power may be a combination of these rhythms, since we are all able to access all of the rhythms. You will have less stress if the greater portion of your life is experienced from your Point of Power. Other rhythms can be tolerated as long as you listen to your frequency for static and interference, and then quickly return to your natural station, avoiding a crisis of conflicting or overwhelming rhythms that are unnatural to you.

You are *designed* with power to be healthy and happy. Any time you move away from that power source (even slightly off your station's frequency) through distortion, changes in life will give you the opportunity to get back on your exact Point of Power. This healing of the break from naturalness works all the time, whether you're aware of it or not.

All life on Earth is involved with light and sound. We can consciously recognize our involvement with light and sound, through our participation with electricity. We have created machines that give us visual information about the electricity in our bodies, such as the bio-feedback machine and the electrocardiogram. Bio-feedback gives us a greater understanding of how our minds affect and change the electrical movement in our bodies.

As a human you are much more than just a physical body. You are blessed with a mental body, an emotional body and a Spiritual body. You use all of these bodies all of the time whether you are conscious of their existence in your life or not. If you are not conscious of your other bodies, you are not experiencing an intimate relationship with your own wholeness, your Soul, the eternal part of you.

Your Spiritual body encompasses all the coding and memory of all life beyond form. The part of you that is eternal. The part of you that is the perfect expression of unconditional love. The part of you that embraces your Soul throughout eternity. The part of you that is the breath of Divine Order waiting to be breathed into your humanness. The unlimited reverence for all life. The recognition of life in all things. Your Oneness, beyond your brain, that lives in your heart, ever ready to be born anew.

Your Spiritual body needs a vehicle for expression in the third dimension, so you have a physical body. The physical body is the stereo supreme. The perfect Divine Instrument to receive the messages of your Oneness from the Spiritual body and your Soul. The physical body is a living sound system and has the ability to hear the sound beyond the sound that your ears register. The physical body can register sound as a sensation from the Universe without having to understand it in order to hear it. This sound will come in as a vibration that creates a sensation or feeling in your body. We can learn to hear these sensations/vibrations the same as we learned to hear verbal language and interpret it in order to communicate with other people. This sound, beyond the sound our ears hear, is the way we expand our ability to communicate with our Soul. Thus you *hear* many sounds of life you do not consciously register or recognize. Your physical body is truly a Temple for the Divine.

Your Spiritual body is formless and can have form and expression through your physical body. In order to give direction to this unity of creation you have a mental body. Your mental body gives you the capacity to function in this third dimension through decisions and choices you make to give direction and expression to your life. Through the mental body, you have the ability to see the world of form through your eyes, the beauty of this Earth and all living things. The mental body, given permission to go beyond limiting beliefs, will always guide you to your Soul, since all your bodies have one destination: ONENESS.

Your emotional body registers the "passion of creation" as the power of the Universe and provides the energy for your physical and mental bodies to use to create movement here in the third dimension. Your emotions are truly the Universal fuel to keep you going as a human being in the world of form. As a soul, when you agree to come to the Earth School, one of the primary reasons is to work on refining and clearing your emotional body of any distortion or residue you may have created by your beliefs or behaviors that are out of harmony with the Divine Plan. Your emotional body is your Gateway to your Soul. When you allow your life to go beyond fear and all of its distortions, the Gateway to your Soul is accessed through the Law of Love. No matter what you are feeling, your Soul is always calling you home. The more conscious you become of your emotions and how you can use this Universal fuel for your journey Home, the more abiding joy you will experience in your daily life.

Just as electricity is always available in the universe in some form, and it is captured for use and transmitted into the physical world, so it is with your Soul. The Essence of who you are is always available in the Universe, whether captured, or not, in a physical, mental or emotional body. The Soul is always alive.

When you, an individual spark of the great electrical field, the Great Source, choose to come to school on the Earth plane you need a vehicle to use while you are here. The vehicle you recognize is a physical body. The mental body is the steering wheel, and the emotional body provides the power for movement for your journey as a Soul on Earth. You have come to this Earth School to experience a deeper level of love, through an intimate relationship with your human self and your Soul.

As a soul, you are co-creator with Spirit of your body, because, when you made your choices to come to this Earth School, you were prepared to evolve your personalized spark to the highest level of expression, in the Divine Plan, with Spirit. Thus, you take this course of Life, with the prerequisites of exactly what you, as a Soul, recognize you need to learn. In your human state, you are love, no matter what your behavior is.

Your journey through this Earth School is for a greater integration of your Eternal Soul Self with your human self. Through your daily experiences, the bridge that unites these two realities, or expressions of life, is Love.

Love is the vehicle that captures your Soul's Essence and continues to transmit it into the receiver, your body. And Love *always* returns your Soul to the Great Source, for more eternal breath, for you to live as a Divine Human on this Earth.

The more you allow yourself to live through Love, as Love, the more you give your humanness permission to be alive. This creates the opportunity for communion, the union, the Divine Marriage of your Soul and your Body. The ultimate class in the Earth School is Oneness. We are all working toward a Degree as a Divine Human Being, expressing our Soul as Light and Love through our daily life.

Your body has been created as a perfect instrument, to receive the spark of Life and is a perfect instrument to distribute the sound of Life. You were born carrying the true sound for your path of Life. You can hear the finest, most sophisticated sound systems on the planet and none compares with your body's ability to receive and deliver light and sound.

One of the reasons for lack of appreciation for our bodies as Divine instruments and receivers/senders of light and sound, is that we are unconscious to most of the light and sound our bodies receive and transmit every day. However, we are becoming more conscious! We are awakening to our Soul sound of Life, once again.

Your Point of Power is a "Sound of your Soul" in the physical world. Awakening to this Divine frequency within your body, mind and emotions, will release a new level of joy, freedom and creativity in your life.

In an orchestra, there are different sections of instruments, which when played together create the sound of the symphony. In your physical body there are different vibrations, which, given their natural expression, will create the sound of your Soul in your daily life. This sound of your Soul, your Point of Power, will be a feeling in your body, similar to the feelings you can experience when you listen to music.

You have different rhythms in your body that register and express your creativity. You can use all these rhythms. There is a rhythm that is strongest for you and allows your creativity to be delivered easily, clearly and powerfully. If you are a member of an orchestra, you may have experience with several instruments and yet choose to play one instrument because that is the one you like the most or feel strongest and most qualified playing. So it is with your Point of Power. You are familiar and know how to experience all of your frequencies/sounds, and there is a rhythm or movement in life that truly allows your naturalness to come forth easily and powerfully when you "play out your life" from that section of your Soul, most of the time.

In an orchestra, it takes all the sections working together to create the full sound of the symphony. The same is true in our bodies. We use all of our frequencies all the time and our power and peace increase as we allow more of our Point of Power, our strongest sound, to come forth more each day in all of our activities. You are living these frequencies now and have been since you were born. Point of Power offers you another view of your creativity so you can expand your personal expression of your Soul through the choices you make, based on more awareness of your Divinity.

You have many expressions of the sound of your Soul—your voice, your walk, your body movement, the way your mind creates and the way you perceive life. The essence of all your expression in life comes from the Soul, and your experiences may have taught you to mask and hide your Essence from most areas of your life.

As you read the information about your Point of Power, you'll recognize another view of your Naturalness/Essence, because you are the living expression of your Point of Power. I am providing some input for your use, as a way to expand your relationship with your Soul. You are in that Divine relationship now. The words in this book do not create that relationship; they merely ignite new illumination from the Star you are, in your movie of Life.

As a Soul, you agreed to come to this Earth stage, and deliver your Greatest Self. Everyone becomes a Star on this stage, and it is your time to shine. The stage is set, the lights are on. Life is ready to receive your Greatest Self.

So why hesitate to deliver your part? What is your part? Why stay backstage, when it is time to be onstage in life? And onstage may not be as in the movies you see, but, by making choices, you are alive and participating more consciously in your own life every day. THE CHOICES YOU MAKE CREATE THE RESULTS YOU LIVE WITH.

When you choose, as a Soul, to enter the Earth School, you choose to come and deliver your Essence. The Earth is more dense than your Soul, and is polluted with thoughts and behaviors that humans have created and deposited, during their journeys here, while seeking the way Home.

You are on Earth as a Soul practicing your divinity in the human role, in the third dimension. Your humanness veiled your memory of the most direct route Home, when you accepted the responsibility of a conscious mind.

So the key is to go through the veils of illusion, and awaken to your Soul's choice for coming to the Earth School. Then practice delivering your part, your sound, until you feel the joy of your part in your present life.

When the student is ready, the teacher will appear. Life is the teacher. You just need to show up in class (LIFE) and be responsible for your choices, so you can experience the communion and marriage of your Soul and your human self. As you awaken to the multi-facets of your Soul, you can make clearer choices on how to deliver your light and sound, as a Divine human being on Earth.

YOU CAN ALWAYS CHOOSE AGAIN. If your perfor-
mance in life feels unrewarding, and lacks fulfillment, love or
joy, you can choose again. You do not have to live the same
script all your life. By recognizing that your choices create beliefs
that affect your behavior, you can change the way you live, by
changing your choices. We are all awakening together; each
person, in his own way, is making his Divine contribution to the
big movie of Life.

Through life's conditioning and experiences, most of us create beliefs and behaviors that lessen the expression of our creative
rhythm. These beliefs and behaviors are in opposition to free-
moving energy, joy and wellness, forcing our lives to function
through stress and distortion of our Points of Power. To reduce
stress, you need to change the beliefs and behaviors that distort
your Point of Power, begin remembering who you are, and transmit
your natural rhythm.

When you use your conscious mind to continue to support
beliefs that are too small for you, that are in conflict with your
Soul, that perpetuate fear rather than love, that thrive on judgments, comparisons, or blame etc., you create and experience
physical and emotional distress. These mind beliefs affect your
nervous system and that creates static that interferes with your
clear reception of your Soul frequency. You may experience this
static as nervousness, irritation, anger, frustration, impatience,
resentment, despair or fear. Just as static on the radio makes it difficult to hear the sound clearly, so static in your nervous system
makes it difficult to hear your Soul sound.

Those feelings are clues to you. You have abandoned your
Divine Essence and you need to listen to that part of you, through
the clear channel of your Soul. That is achieved by changing your
behavior, your environment, your relationships or whatever you
have created that is limiting your full Self-expression. Return to
your Point of Power and allow your natural rhythm to once again
be free. You will know when you are "on station," your physical
body will begin to relax, you will breathe easier and deeper, you
will feel less frustration and less mental pressure. All your bodies—
mental, physical, emotional and spiritual—respond quickly when
you allow your Point of Power to be used in your life.

You are divinely designed with power to be healthy and happy. Any time you move away from that power source (even slightly off your station's frequency) through distortions created by your belief system, changes in life will give you the opportunity to get back on your exact Point of Power. This healing of the break from naturalness goes on all the time, whether you are aware of it or not. Your autonomic nervous system is designed to support life, at a foundational level, and make adjustments necessary to continue life in the body. So does your Soul frequency monitor your energy movement, through your bodies, and maintains the balance with or without your conscious recognition or participation. This Soul monitoring system is present in the physical body, to ensure that there is an avenue open for the Life Force to easily and consistently enter and support the physical body.

If you are unaware of the Soul frequency and sound, one of the ways Life offers you the opportunity to get "back on station" is through an experience we call a crisis. Crisis is a life situation where you drop everything else and focus only on the moment and what is happening in the moment. After the crisis is over, you usually try to get your life in order again. In most cases, the order you're trying to re-establish is the cause of the crisis. That particular situation, lifestyle, behavior, job, relationship or routine was not supporting your Life. The Soul is designed to support Life in the human body, until you refuse to allow your naturalness to breathe and live, because of your fears or decision to release the body, and experience the next step of Life through the process called death.

You can trust your Soul's support in your Life. It has kept you alive and breathing and brought you to this moment. After a crisis, your desire to get your life in order again, according to old habits, beliefs and behaviors, never works. You've out grown and expanded your reality beyond your previous belief system. The older, smaller system simply doesn't fit you any longer. A crisis gives you the opportunity to create another reality—one that embraces more of your true Essence. As you accept this expansion in your life, you'll feel less static/stress in your body. With less static, you're in more of your naturalness, on frequency, to your own Sound. When you're on frequency, your life is filled with balance, clarity and peace.

Just as the tree is composed of roots, trunk, branches and leaves to make a complete creation, we have four distinct frequencies we receive and distribute through our human bodies. The tree has to have all its four aspects to be whole, and you are able to access those four frequencies in your body, to create wholeness and balance.

Your Point of Power is one of the frequencies of your Soul's expression. A tree represents how your Point of Power moves through your life and how you use it on a daily basis, through the Roots, Trunk, Branches and Leaves. Each of these four frequencies is an active creator, and your Point of Power may be a combination of these frequencies, since we are all able to access all of the frequencies. You will have less stress if 80% of each day is experienced from your Point of Power. Other frequencies can be tolerated, but if you receive static or interference, return to your "natural station," and avoid a crisis of conflicting or overwhelming rhythms that are unnatural to you. Your nervous system was designed to function best when participating in life, at your Point of Power, most of the time. Your Point of Power is your place of Excellence, a balance and rhythm for the mental, physical, emotional, and spiritual Self.

The trees on our planet are our Guardians of Breath. Your physical body is Guardian of your Soul for your Earth journey. (See illustration 1.)

Leaves • Visionary

conscious	unconscious
ideas	unrealistic
concepts	evasive
vision	judgmental
initiation	disassociated
challenge	impractical
movement	impatient

(formless)

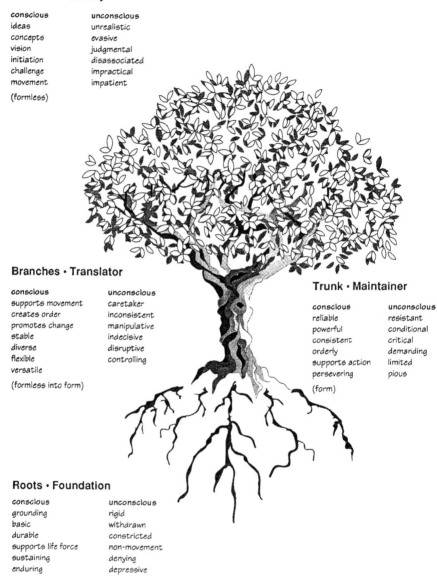

Branches • Translator

conscious	unconscious
supports movement	caretaker
creates order	inconsistent
promotes change	manipulative
stable	indecisive
diverse	disruptive
flexible	controlling
versatile	

(formless into form)

Trunk • Maintainer

conscious	unconscious
reliable	resistant
powerful	conditional
consistent	critical
orderly	demanding
supports action	limited
persevering	pious

(form)

Roots • Foundation

conscious	unconscious
grounding	rigid
basic	withdrawn
durable	constricted
supports life force	non-movement
sustaining	denying
enduring	depressive

(form)

ILLUSTRATION 1   As you claim your Point of Power you can capture the energy of the unconscious attributes and refocus that power consciously.

Your ROOTS frequency is "foundational," sustaining life through growth, change, balance and regeneration as part of your life system. Your Soul taps into the life force/breath of the Earth, and magnetizes this energy into your body, nurturing life at a deep level of your Being.

Your frequency of the TRUNK is the "maintainer." This frequency is solid, strong, consistent and powerful in supporting the movement of life through order and systems in life. The balance in your daily life is referenced through this frequency. When you are in fear or crisis, you will use this Point of Power as your safe place, to return to familiar patterns and behavior, until you can expand your movement once again, safely.

Your BRANCH frequency is the "translator." The power of this frequency brainstorms ideas, translating these ideas into form—projects, organizations, etc. When the project is up and running, you will want to turn this project over to a Trunk person or a system that can maintain it, and start another project. This is the connecting energy, the part of you that takes an idea (formless) and brings it into form. Like a branch of a tree, this frequency connects the idea with the support system.

The LEAVES represent the "visionary" part of you. As a visionary, your mind receives thoughts, pictures and ideas, every day, that are as numerous as leaves on a tree. Your favorite way to live as a Leaf is to keep moving with your body and mind. Doing more than one thing at a time, having several projects happening at the same time and many options in life, are inspiring for the Leaves.

Chapter 2

Dance with Your Tree of Life

Self Assessment Tool to Discover
Your Point of Power

By listening to your "voice of avoidance"—the part of you that keeps saying,—"You need to get this done!", "Why didn't you do this yet?", "You should have completed this yesterday!"—you may discover areas in your life that need support or recognition so these parts of you can deliver your naturalness easily. You can increase your confidence and learn to do many, many things easily and well through your own Self-acceptance and recognition of what is natural and supportive for you.

Many times *avoidance* is a clue, a messenger from your Divine Essence, that what you *think* you should do is not your naturalness and may be difficult to undertake, especially if it is motivated by judgment from your internal or external Authority figure. Avoidance usually indicates an area where you feel weak or lack confidence in your abilities; therefore you do not want to set yourself up for failure or rejection, so you avoid the experience.

The following is a self assessment tool to explore some areas in your life where you may have been avoiding experiences and thus reducing your expression of joy and creativity in life:

Using a scale from 1 to 5, 1 being not very often and 5 being often, rate yourself on the following statements. Then add up the numbers and total each section separately. The totals will give you an idea where your Point of Power is strongest and what other areas of the tree support your Point of Power and to what degree. (The higher numbers, in any section, indicate your natural participation with this rhythm.)

Chapter 2/ Self Assessment Tool

LEAVES

I   II

— — I have lots of ideas that never get completed.

— — I have difficulty staying focused during conversations.

— — It is easy and fun for me to do more than one thing at a time.

— — I have concerns about making commitments for fear I'll miss out on something else, or I'll have to be responsible for that commitment.

— — I'm fearful of sharing my ideas with others because they think I am unrealistic.

— — Many times I leave a trail of unfinished projects as I move through the day (laundry, painting, lawn care, etc).

BRANCHES

I   II

— — After I create something, I begin to lose interest in it.

— — I'm always open and looking for my next "new project."

— — I like to have freedom to create in my own way and at my own pace.

— — When I am involved in a project I am open to new input and ideas, as long as I am not required to follow other ideas to the exclusion of my own.

— — I can be interrupted and maintain and return to my focus.

— — Some people consider me inconsistent in my work world.

Chapter 2/Self Assessment Tool

TRUNK

I   II

— — I resent being interrupted in my projects.

— — I like to do things "my way."

— — I need to experience change in my life at a slow, steady pace to feel safe.

— — I like consistency in my life.

— — It is fun for me to put the details of life together in an orderly way.

— — I like having a schedule in my life.

ROOTS

I   II

— — I like to be by myself with the earth and nature.

— — I like to observe and live life, not philosophize about it.

— — People accuse me of being rude, stubborn and uncommunicative.

— — I like to live simply.

— — I like to go about my day undisturbed.

— — There is a lot more to my feeling nature than most people realize.

Now go through and do this assessment again on how **YOU REALLY FEEL**—not how you have been taught to respond in life based on what you think others expect of you. Is there a difference? What did you discover about you? If there is a difference, how much effect do you think and feel this has on your daily decisions in your life?

This is a speedy way to assess your Point of Power from observing some of the behaviors you are familiar with in your daily life. There is another self assessment tool that you can use that provides information from your subconscious. This is done through the following visualization process. I would suggest using both methods of assessment and see what information they provide for you.

POINT OF POWER VISUALIZATION

This visualization will be done from a conscious state of awareness. Just close your eyes and allow your mind to deliver whatever images come up. Do not edit what your mind presents. There is no right or wrong way to do this. It does not need to make sense. Nothing needs to match. Just observe and report or record whatever is presented.

Ask someone to read this to you, allowing you to experience this visualization process. They may record your information as you describe your creation to them, or you may be silent the whole time you go through the whole visualization and, later, record what you saw. It may be easier for you to draw your vision than put it into words.

The following information needs to be given slowly, with time for you to describe what you are seeing as you go along, if you are having an assistant record the details for you.

Now close your eyes and make yourself comfortable, and take some deep breaths. As you breathe in and out, visualize this breath going through your mind and allowing your mind to be clearer and clearer, just as the breeze blows away the clouds. Allow your breath to clear away your confusion, stress and the mind's chatter. Just allow your mind to come to a quiet place.

In that quiet and clear place, I would like you to create an **EMPTY ROOM**, and describe that empty room aloud. (Pause for visualizer to respond.)

Next, create the **BASE OF A TABLE**, the bottom part only, and describe it. (Pause) Now place a **TOP** on that table, and verbally express what you've created. (Pause) Now create a **VASE**, and place the vase on the table. Describe your vase. (Pause) Tap on the vase. Does it make a sound? If so, what does it sound like? (Pause) Now place a **FLOWER** in the vase. (Pause) Then make a bouquet. (Pause) Can you smell the flowers? (Pause) Do you recognize the fragrance? (Pause) Now **WATER** the bouquet, and tell how you do that. (Pause)

Look around the room you've created—your creative laboratory. You can have this room any way you want it, so make any **ADDITIONS** or changes, anything you want, until this room feels exactly the way you want it to feel. (Pause) Now, how does it feel to you? (Pause) What's your experience in this room you've created? (Pause)

You can have access to this room any time you want merely by bringing your mind back to this place. You can do anything you want with your mind in this special place. You can recreate this room in any way you want, at any time, by merely closing your eyes. The feeling you experience here can go with you in your daily life—by recognizing it, by experiencing it, and by allowing it to come with you. Do that right now.

Surrounded in that very special energy, return your awareness to the room you're physically in, and open your eyes when you're ready.

How did you feel as you answered the above questions?

ANALYZING YOUR VISUALIZATION

A LEAF Point of Power will have lengthy notes, perhaps pages. Because visionaries are constantly creating and recreating, their imagery changes as they work with it, which requires a lot of words to express. The room and the experiences that Leaves create won't always be something that can actually be reproduced in a practical way. For example, a visionary's room may have no walls or ceiling, only a floor. Leaves may have difficulty staying with one image per word, and may precede the process—have a bouquet before the direction is given. Their minds naturally create without instructions being given. Their favorite place to dwell, mentally, is formless, without structure.

A BRANCH Point of Power won't be as verbose or changeable in describing his or her room. Branches are very creative and flexible in their creation. Their images will change, depending on the amount of visionary capacity they embody. A Branch usually creates a room of movement, open space, etc. This room is generally reproducible in this dimension, although a wall may be missing or there may be no ceiling. Branches love to touch base with the formless world of vision and translate this vision into this reality of form.

The information and responses from a TRUNK are much more direct and concise. A Trunk's images are very real, and usually solid, as we experience them in our daily lives. Trunks respond to the guidelines of the process, and may have some distress if their images don't seem to match or go together.

Rarely will a ROOTS Point of Power choose to be in a situation where he or she may be asked to do this process. Roots people are not interested in pursuing life through their minds. They live through their senses. Their desire in life is to live simply. The Root part of you will usually show up in your visualization through some aspect of nature, such as a wooden table, clay vase, wild flowers.

The **ROOM** you create represents the consciousness through which your Point of Power, your naturalness, is delivered. Notice the amount of light you allow in this room. This indicates your mental openness to change and your inner state of mind at this time. This room and light level may change each time you experience this visualization.

The **BASE OF THE TABLE** relates to the level of your individual security, how you receive support, based on how solid you make the base of your table, what you make it of, and whether it's more abstract or more fragile. So the more solid the base, the more you need a solid foundation, structure and guidelines in your life. This represents the Trunk and Root part in you. The more fragile or ornate, or refined the base, the more Leaf and Branch rhythm is in you.

The **TOP** on the table is just another aspect of completion. One way this relates is determining if the top has any matching correlation to the base—if so, it indicates Trunk or Branch characteristics. If the table top is totally abstract, if it keeps changing, if it doesn't match the base at all, or if you want to change the base, that indicates a Branch going into Leaf modality. Notice the detail, or lack of detail, in the table. This indicates your conscious use of detail in whatever Point of Power you are.

The **VASE** gives some indication of the level of support that three-dimensional things provide. If the shape is heavier on the bottom, then there's the need again for some foundation, guidelines, support, some security—at a very strong, root level—depicting a Trunk and Root tendency. If the vase is translucent, refined glass, opaque, ornately decorated, if it keeps changing, it represents a Branch to Leaf movement.

Tapping the vase, hearing it or not can demonstrate whether you're auditory or kinesthetic, because kinesthetic people, even with their eyes closed, will literally raise their hands and look like they're tapping something. Auditory people usually tilt their heads a bit to the side, and listen.

If you're living as a Trunk when, in fact, you're a Leaf, it may be revealed in this part of the visualization. You will create or change in ways that are uncommon to you in your daily life. You will create something you haven't seen or don't know. Allow yourself this exploration. It could be the beginning of a whole new expression of your true Self.

Some of the areas that will give you a clue if your Point of Power is different than your behavior based on your belief system are the vase, flower, bouquet and watering of the flowers. Example: If you have been trained, or trained yourself, to think and behave as a Trunk or Branch, the first part of your visualization will reflect this. At any one of the areas symbolized by the vase, flower, bouquet or watering, a visual may show up that is something you would *never think of doing or creating*. This will give you a clue, you may be confining your Point of Power through limited beliefs about your creativity.

You were asked to place a **FLOWER** in the vase. Leaves will rarely place a single flower; it's immediately a **BOUQUET**. Then they try to get it back to just a single flower. A Trunk or Branch will most likely place a flower in the vase. The Trunk rhythm will always wait for the next instruction on performing this imagery. The Leaf, even though waiting for guidelines, is still creating with the last piece of information received, or is jumping ahead, then will change the flower or flowers. The Trunk will always keep the original flower in the bouquet. This is not always true for the Branches; sometimes they will and sometimes they won't.

In asking you to smell the flower or bouquet, we're checking out the senses. A Trunk or Branch, who is aware of the flowers' fragrance, most of the time will smell the fragrance that corresponds to that type of flower or bouquet. A Leaf bouquet can be anything, and the fragrance can be whatever it is—it doesn't have to associate with the visual representation.

WATERING the bouquet is a clear demarcation point, because it reveals what type of individual creativity is present, whether you're a combination Point of Power or aligned with a specific one. If the instrument for watering just appears, filled with water, then you're probably a Branch. If it just appears and is unlike anything you've ever seen, or if you water the bouquet in a very different way—maybe not using an instrument, water may drip from mid-air—then you're probably a Leaf. If you go to the kitchen and get the instrument, fill it with water, bring it back to your room, lift up the flowers and pour in the water, then you're a Trunk with very little Branch influence.

Double-check these places for potential change: the vase, flower, bouquet and watering. The vase begins that change if you have more than just one Point of Power.

When you make additions to your room, it also shows whether or not you are a combination of energies or a concentration of one. The reason I refer most often in this process to Leaf, Branches and Trunk is that Roots don't usually participate in this kind of process. My experience with them is usually personal, not as clients. Since the Roots live predominantly through their experiences, rather than their mental processes, they determine their Point of Power by just living it. Trunk rhythm will participate in this type of process if you explain very clearly what it is, how you're going to do it and what their part is, and that there's no right or wrong, no judgment and nothing has to match. If it's clearly defined, they then have confidence to participate. Branches think it's fun, and Leaves live like this, so it's natural for them.

Regarding **ADDITIONS** in the room, a Trunk, will wait to be asked, "Is there anything else you'd like to add?" In order to make changes, Trunks may have to be given permission, be asked a question, or be supported that it's okay to continue. Branches will begin the process and continue until they get what they want. The only difficulty Leaves have is stopping making changes and additions. They can go on for hours, so I give them the opportunity to present their information and make changes until I think that room is comfortable for them. Then I ask, "How do you feel in this room? Is this a room you like?"

Now, review Illustration 1 and assess your Point of Power. Which part of the tree do you recognize represents the area you feel most natural in? Where do you have more enthusiasm and creativity and less stress and resistance? You're not confined to one modality.

Next, see Illustration 2 for some possible combinations and determine which most accurately expresses your Point of Power, or draw your own line that you feel combines the rhythms that comprise your Point of Power. Based on your assessment, begin to be a conscious observer of your life, and allow your Point of Power to be alive and breathing daily, wherever you are.

I grew up behaving as a Trunk rhythm with some Branch rhythm. This was learned behavior, not my naturalness. It took me years and this information to really begin to understand that my naturalness is Branch and Leaf rhythm. Even after learning this, sometimes I still have to practice releasing my old conditioning and allowing myself to participate easily in my own naturalness. The more I practice this, the easier it becomes. The blessing of having learned strong Trunk behaviors and skills is that I can use these skills now in my life to support me in many ways and actually free up the Leaf part of me to be even more creative.

One possibility to keep in mind: I have worked with a few

Leaves who taught themselves to behave as Trunks in order to survive, gain approval from others and feel okay about themselves. When they discovered their Point of Power was actually as a visionary, it created a radical change in their reality and lifestyle. Trunk people feel they are losing control of their lives when they begin to explore their Point of Power as a Leaf. This requires so much trust, as they allow their visionary self to have a greater priority in their daily life. Releasing the need to know all the details from start to finish and how everything is going to happen, will allow an easier transition from Trunk behavior to Visionary movement.

Allowing the naturalness of the visionary to emerge is a very challenging experience, especially from the conditioning in our society which promotes limitations of our naturalness, rather than acceptance and appreciation. It is very helpful to have a friend or counselor as a reference point in life as you go through this change. Love, support and understanding make this transition possible with a minimum of discomfort. The behavior and skills learned by functioning as a Trunk can definitely be redirected and incorporated as an asset for a Leaf.

One thing to remember: as a Leaf, you always want to make changes happen immediately. After all, that is how your vision creates the ideas you see, instantly. This is one process where patience will be your biggest support. Use the Trunk strength, of one step at a time, to support your releasing the beliefs and limitations you have experienced in your life. As you allow this change to take place gradually, it makes integration much easier. There is a great benefit for any Leaf who has functioned as a Trunk; you have learned procedures that you can always call upon to support your daily life.

No matter what your Point of Power, when you are fearful or in crisis, you will always respond to life as a Trunk person, wanting life to slow down, make sense and feel safer. You return to habits, behaviors and beliefs you have known and used the longest. Just as the Trunk of the tree supports the Life Force moving through the tree, so the Trunk part of you contains the guidelines and familiar places you want to return to and experience, when you feel unsafe or threatened by changes in your life. You will remain in this mode until changes occur and you once again begin to feel safe. As your

Illustration 2

POINT OF POWER RHYTHMS

Do Any Of These Represent Your Point Of Power?
If Not, Use The Blank Chart And Draw Your Own Representation

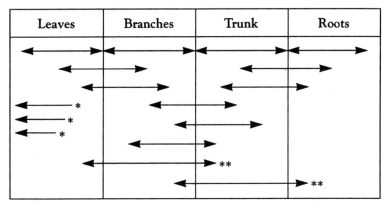

Leaves	Branches	Trunk	Roots

*These are Leaves who basically have a minimal relationship with implementation—they may appear confused, when in fact they are living in a more formless reality than many others. They truly have difficulty functioning in a mundane, daily life.

**A person may have a point of power that extends through three rhythms. These point of power combinations are created by rhythms that are adjacent.

Chart Your Own Rhythm Below

Leaves	Branches	Trunk	Roots

fears lift, you will allow yourself to expand and return to your natural rhythm, your Point of Power.

Leaves behaving as Trunks is the only interchange of rhythms I've seen in the years I've worked with Points of Power. The other modalities seem to remain consistent. As you accept your Point of Power, you can let go of other people's expectations of you. You don't have to live up to someone else's vision of how your life should be. You can release expectations of yourself and allow yourself to participate in life from your own joy and excitement. Life sure feels a lot easier when you drop the judgments you are holding on yourself. And an amazing thing happens, as you release judgments on yourself, you begin to release the need to judge others.

When you begin to consciously recognize your naturalness and appreciate yourself, you can become more accepting of all the rhythms available in each Point of Power. Then determine the areas of your life where, if strengthened, you could feel more balanced and less stressed in your life.

I have discovered, if I can spend about 80% of my day expressing in my Point of Power, the other 20% I can spend in the other rhythms and still feel very balanced, on most days. Physical tiredness, emotional upsets, or mental stress influences my adaptability on a moment to moment basis, no matter what my focus or Point of Power is. You will discover, the more you can live your life from your naturalness, the more energy you will have.

If it appears you are spending less then 80 per cent of your day in your Point of Power—your natural rhythm—this would definitely be a contributing factor to your physical, mental and emotional stress. With this awareness, you can consciously observe your participation in relationships, employment and daily routines and, choose again to create a lifestyle that you consciously design to clearly express who you really are. As you experience this new lifestyle, you will discover your whole outside world begins to feel different, even if it looks the same.

Let's explore the Point of Power Tree of Life and see how you can expand your freedom of expression, by embracing all parts of yourself.

ROOTS

If your Point of Power is Roots, you can see there is a lot of distance between the Roots and the Leaves. As a Root, you must incorporate some air and sunshine in your life. The more you can expose yourself to people and activities that bring a different energy or experience into your life, the more you fertilize your own depth and growth. It does not mean you have to participate at gatherings and be the life of the party. Just be present in your own Point of Power. Taking yourself into these new adventures of life is nurturing and expanding for you, even though it may not feel that way at the time.

Once you realize your naturalness and who you truly are, you may discover a great deal of joy in meeting other people and experiencing new situations. You can also release the judgment on yourself and how you should behave. An amazing thing happens: as you release the judgment on you—less judgment comes back to you from others.

As a Root, you will probably appreciate the solid people more, those who are pretty "down to earth," the Trunks of the world. You may actually be comfortable participating in a business or social way with Trunk people and having fun. Branch people, or experiencing the Branch part of yourself, is going to S-T-R-E-T-C-H you more than your Trunk relationships. This part of life involves some element of the unknown, a less defined reality, and seems to change often. This is a good time to remember that your silence is your power, and there is no need to talk unless you have something you want to say. Accept your Roots as your naturalness and increase your sense of confidence and trust in who you are.

For a Root to have any lengthy, intimate relationship with a Leaf would require a great deal of compassion and patience on both parts. There is a lot of difference between the roots and leaves on a tree, and yet they are both essential to the tree.

A Root person would probably enjoy a Leaf person as a stand-up comedian more than a friend. The way a Leaf person communicates may be difficult for a Root person, since the Leaf has so many ideas at one time, they have a difficult time getting the words out of their mouth in sequence and rarely finish their sentences.

TRUNK

As a Trunk Point of Power, it is usually easy and natural to go deeper inside yourself through your participation with nature (swimming, hiking, listening to and moving with music, etc.) to access your Roots, the foundational part of you. You have much in common with Root persons. You feel comfortable with them. You may experience deep, meaningful, fulfilling relationships with them.

Your connection with the Branch part of you may not feel as comfortable as with your Roots. Branches introduce change, transition, increased options, less structure in your life and the need to be spontaneous with less information than Trunks usually like to have. This association can also be very inspiring, challenging and stimulating.

You may feel more comfortable with small doses of Branch activity in your life. When these options are presented, it will feel much safer and easier to choose if you are given clear, concise and complete information on these choices. Bringing too many unknown, undefined options into your life can feel frustrating or overwhelming.

In relating to the Leaves, you may like watching these people or activities or playing with them once in a while but you can feel frustrated and unable to accomplish much with them. They never seem to make a decision and just do it. They always change their minds. Thus, when you access the Leaf part of yourself, you have trouble accepting your ideas, images and visions, as real, or possible, or even desirable.

If you can envision it, everything is possible for all Points of Power, based on your willingness and courage to embrace the Leaf part of yourself, the Visionary, Free Spirit part of you.

When you participate with the Leaves or Leaf part of you, stay open to new possibilities in your life, release your conditions on how situations have to look or feel and allow yourself to feel safe and explore these new experiences, even if it does take you out of your comfort zone. You can always choose again and return to familiar patterns and relationships that feel safe and supportive, if these new experiences seem too challenging.

BRANCHES

As a Branch, on the Tree of Life, you are in a great position to directly access Vision (Leaves) or stability (Trunk). The only part of the Tree you do not access directly is the Roots. A Branch must have active and daily participation with Leaves. From the Leaves come the ideas, visions, possibilities to create with. The Leaves constantly spark new ideas for you as a Branch. As these ideas begin to take shape and become organized then you want to participate with the Trunk, the Maintainer, who provides supportive energy for your creation.

You may encounter some frustration when it is time to participate with the sequential details of the project (Trunk), if you are still in high gear with the Vision (Leaf) part of your creation. You appreciate the stable part of progress as you see your vision develop before your eyes.

Your connection as a Branch with the Roots must come as a conscious choice. You will usually use this energy as a place to regenerate, recharge and regroup before you enter your next project. It is very important to remember to do this, because as a Branch you usually get so immersed in your projects that you forget to take a break and take care of yourself until it's over. Because you are always looking for the next project, as you feel the present one "winding down," you easily get involved in the new creation and overlook your Roots, the part that sustains life, our foundation and connection with the earth.

LEAVES

As a Leaf, you have access to the universe through your visions. Since your naturalness is a Visionary, you always have playmates, in your imagination. You may feel alone, in this world of vision, or very much "at home." In your everyday life, you may feel misunderstood or that you do not have much in common with those around you. What you recognize and see regularly does not exist consciously in many people's reality.

You will usually appreciate and be appreciated by the Branch people in your life. They seem to be able to understand you, and you can even carry on a conversation with each other, most of the time. How much of a visionary you are will determine how easy or difficult it will be be for you to access and use your own Branch power. (See Illustration 2.) The farther out on a limb you are as a Leaf the more difficulty you will have in translating/experiencing your life with any other part of the Tree, inside or outside of you. Being with other Leaves is like being on vacation; you can relax and just visualize and verbalize. Branches will usually be easy to communicate with because they are close to your Point of Power.

To appreciate Trunk people, or your own Trunk abilities, you will have to make a conscious choice to do so. You will need to reduce your mental speed or increase your patience, in order to participate in conversation with a Trunk rhythm, in you or another person. Leaves are sometimes critical of the Trunk move-ment in themselves or others, as being too slow, not listening or not understanding. In the Tree of Life, the Branches are the bridge between the Leaves and the Trunk. If this is not consciously rec-ognized and appreciated as a unique and necessary difference, con-tinuous conflict, judgment, frustration and projection take place between Leaves and Trunk people. All parts of the tree are essen-tial for balance.

Most Leaves create some kind of a connection with the Root part of themselves—they need to feel grounded and maintain a point of balance in their lives. Some of the ways I have seen Leaves use their Roots are gardening, surfing, swimming, making pottery, hiking, cycling and running. Once leaves are grounded, they can return to the universe and their visions and feel safe again. Relationships between Leaves and Roots are usually on a casual or business basis and can be quite beneficial for both parties.

We encompass all parts on the TREE OF LIFE, and the more we can expand and embrace all these parts of ourselves and grow in acceptance, gratitude and appreciation for those around us, the fuller our life will be and the stronger our sense of freedom and balance.

CHAPTER 3
Roots • Foundation

conscious	unconscious
grounding	rigid
basic	withdrawn
durable	constricted
supports life force	non-movement
sustaining	denying
enduring	depressive

(form)

As you claim your Point of Power you can capture the energy of the unconscious attributes and refocus that power consciously.

Chapter 3

Roots

Your Roots are your foundational connection to this Earth. They are like a Universal umbilical cord, that feels the pulse of the Earth, through your body. In our culture we have very little training to hear this pulse or the language of this connection with all life through our body.

The indigenous tribes—Native American Indians, Hawaiians, Aborigines and Maoris—lived their daily life through this connection. Their tribes had no conflicting education that taught them to separate from their naturalness. Even though in many parts of the world we have lost this rhythm on a conscious level, the message is still present in each of us.

The Roots rhythm is like gravity. Although we can't see gravity, we live under its law, whether we believe in it or not. Likewise, seeing or believing in this sound of life is not what validates its effect on our life. The blessing of awakening to the Roots rhythm is that we get to consciously feel more of our aliveness. We experience less separation and a stronger connection with all life. This can increase our sense of safety in our daily life.

When you begin to listen and hear the sound of life that lives within, you will naturally create a more intimate, conscious relationship with your body. The body is the temple for your Soul. As you begin your inner journey, you learn how to hear your body through new ways of listening. This listening is really an experience of the sensations that go on in your body that you have no explanation for and yet feel them.

One of the first things we usually do, if we experience some-thing new or unusual in our body, is think something is wrong. Especially if this is an unexplained or unrecognized sensation in our body. When we think something is wrong with our body, our first place we go for support is usually the medical profession. Often these sensations are natural and not signs or symptoms of a disease. Most of the time we are so stressed in our daily life we have no space for this sound of life to be heard. When anything unfamiliar or unusual appears, we have a certain amount of anxiety, fear or confusion come up for us.

As you begin to listen, feel and explore these sensations, you will begin to trust and respect this pulse of life in a new way. You are the only one who can interpret what your body messages mean. Others can share with you their personal experiences and discov-eries. Your experience may be different and still very valid for you. This truly is one of the most exciting, amazing aspects of our inner journey, as we discover a whole new conversation available to us when we learn to listen in a new way. Every part of our body has been designed to support Life. The more we listen to this sound of Life, the more alive we feel.

We can all access this frequency, even if we are not always aware it is supporting our daily lives like roots of a tree or the foundation of a building. With this frequency as your Point of Power, you will excel at living in a simple, efficient, productive lifestyle. When you are hearing the sound of life, the task you are involved in becomes a meditation, and you can easily do the same task for many hours. This is part of the power of the Roots, this deep and abiding peacefulness, one heartbeat with all life.

This part of you is physical, kinesthetic and tactile. You love to have your hands/body involved in the experience. The motiva-tion for movement here is through the senses. The reward is the experience of living life simply. This frequency is in touch with the Earth and the physical dimension. Roots people are efficient and productive, through long hours of participation with a limited variance in the daily life experience.

Roots usually have a close, natural relationship with nature, and will choose to participate in that environment most of the time. If the environment where you live is missing trees, birds, flowers or quiet places, find an area in your neighborhood that feels safe, solid, quiet and peaceful, and visit there regularly. Your naturalness will guide you to these areas, if your busy mind will allow you to listen to you body.

This frequency is essential. Just as the trees release oxygen to sustain our life force, the Roots Point of Power supports life at a foundation level. The natural laws of life are basic, and Roots live from that reality. The communication from a Roots person is simple, direct and concise.

Roots people are comfortable in a lifestyle that doesn't include lots of movement through changes. Consistency in life feels supportive to them, and they support life through their consistent behavior. Living in a foundational reality, Roots don't desire complex, mental philosophies or discussions. They don't feel stimulated through the mind, nearly as much as they feel stimulated through their senses.

When Roots reverse the use of their Point of Power—turn their energy in on themselves—they can behave from a rigid, prejudicial, conditional and limited perspective on life, thereby experiencing restrictions in most areas of their lives.

Functioning with the positive energy of your Point of Power, you experience expansion. When you reverse the use of your Power, and don't express your naturalness, you experience constriction that may appear as physical stress, emotional overload or mental confusion.

As I was growing up, I had a favorite uncle, Uncle John. As a child, I certainly didn't consciously know anything about Point of Power. As I learned about it, I realized Uncle John's Point of Power was the Roots. He was a farmer in Colorado for over fifty years. He had a relationship with the land, the chickens, the animals, the machinery and the plants. Everything grew so well for him, it indicates to me that his frequency was very clear.

Uncle John's relationship with people was equally open and consistent. He was very accepting of others, or silent if he disapproved. Even when he was angry, which was a rare thing for me to see, he rarely said much. He just moved with it, and corrected what needed to be fixed, cleared or changed.

He watched people and life closely. He never missed a thing. I was always curious to hear his observations. Sometimes I asked enough questions, or the right questions, to enter his world of awareness.

His gift to me was his unconditional love. I didn't have to explain me or my life, he knew and accepted me, and just loved me. After Aunt Belle died (they had been married 61 years), Uncle John was very lonely. He was 92. We had great times together, going for long drives, rarely talking, unless he gave me an armchair tour of the history of the countryside, or while we had lunch at the Village Inn Pancake House. This was his favorite place, because they left the coffee pot on the table.

He was an avid baseball fan. His favorite way to "listen" to the game (other than being at the stadium) was to turn on the TV and watch the game, with the sound turned down, and listen to the radio describe the plays. He never missed a thing!

ROOTS

FREQUENCY: Sustaining Movement, nurturing the needs of the physical reality, enduring

SOUND: Earth
Deep, silent and connected to an inner core of life

Body has a pace that is attuned to the Earth. Likes that pace to be undisturbed by outside forces.

DESIRE: Allow life to move naturally
Keep life simple
Walk your talk

GIFT: Connection to our Essence as a Divine Human Being
The part of us that draws in the Life Force from the Earth.

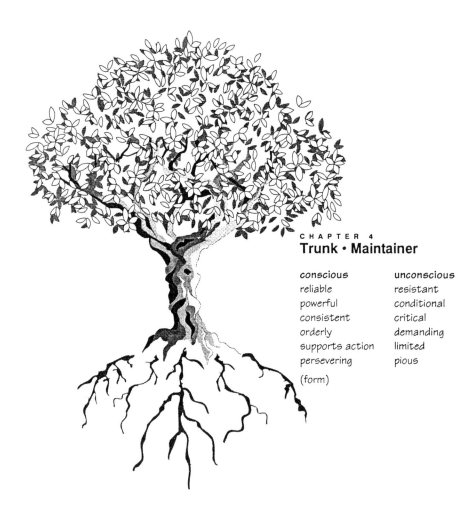

CHAPTER 4
Trunk • Maintainer

conscious	unconscious
reliable	resistant
powerful	conditional
consistent	critical
orderly	demanding
supports action	limited
persevering	pious
(form)	

As you claim your Point of Power you can capture the energy of the unconscious attributes and refocus that power consciously.

Chapter 4

Trunk

The trunk of the tree carries the life force from the roots to the rest of the tree. The Trunk Point of Power maintains the systems that are the life blood for our society: transportation, computer networks, food distribution, and educational systems. These systems support the circulation of information, supplies and food, that allows masses of people to have a sense of order in their daily lives. This is a sustaining, supportive energy, preferring life to be consistent.

As a Trunk person you are motivated by visible accomplishment within an existing system. Your reward and joy is completion, which gives you a sense of fulfillment.

You have an amazing ability to gather the details and arrange them and make sense out of them and even provide a copy for the rest of the world to see and use. You recognize the practical things in life that are essential for life to move. Whatever your passion in life may be, you are loyal to it and persevering. You have the ability to accept the part of Life you star in, and be responsible and reliable in your delivery. You like to have order in your life; it brings you comfort.

If change is coming, you want to be notified ahead of time and given the chance to adjust. There is a tremendous sense of accomplishment when you choose a task and can start this project and complete it without having to make major changes along the way. As a matter of fact, if you could pick up a Blueprint for your Life from the Co-Creator Store, you would feel quite comfortable. You really do like to have a plan for living.

When your life is interrupted over and over and you feel overwhelmed because of all the changes, you may begin to feel depressed, lose confidence in yourself or feel nervous and irritable, feeling there's no way out.

As a Trunk Point of Power, when you are working with a project, you maximize your strength when you are given full details of the project in a clear, concise, consistent manner (usually written) and have the opportunity to ask questions. As soon as you feel you have all the details necessary in the order you want them, you will begin the project. From this point on, your focus is on *completion*. Unless you need additional information, the next thing you will do is complete the project. The natural essence of a Trunk frequency is to have a project, and be able to devote time and energy to make it happen!

Your efficiency and productivity are easily maintained when a project looks possible. Since you are motivated by personal, measurable accomplishment, you persevere as long as you feel you can complete the task. If the project appears to be hopeless for whatever reason, now is a good time to invite others to help you develop options to solve the problems.

There are two essentials when a Trunk person invites others to participate midway in the project: Remember, your reward is the sense of accomplishment upon completion of your project. If you include others before the task is completed, you could easily judge yourself as incompetent, because you couldn't do it by yourself, and the task is not done yet. The other possibility that follows this is, since you like to work by a plan and not be interrupted, it may be difficult to receive others' input and not feel intruded upon. You feel best when the changes that occur in your life seem to be your idea not someone else's.

This is a good time to remember you are just gathering additional information and ideas, and you can make the final decision on how these will be included in the project and choose the people you want to support you. Any time a plan or project is altered midstream, you are not a failure, the project just needs some additional input for completion. Avoid self-judgment when this happens.

If a trunk of a tree was constantly being moved or bent over, this would seriously influence its life. This is true for a Trunk Point of Power, also. Too many changes and interruptions in your life seriously affect your sense of stability and attitude about yourself and life. This is the beginning of emotional overload for you, and can be avoided by understanding your needs and how to support yourself.

Here is a check list you can add to:

1. You don't like to feel pushed around. You want to take life one step at a time.

2. You prefer to initiate change in your life and implement these changes at you own pace.

3. Make lists. This way you can make sure all the questions or information you want is there before you begin your project.

4. Life is about change. When your project is interrupted, you do not have to blame yourself. Interruption is a part of life.

If the project you are working on is revised or changed, you may feel frustrated and irritable, because your natural rhythm has been interrupted. If the interruption is additional information being given to you every few minutes, creating change in a short time, and altering the original plan, this may feel crazy-making to you.

When life brings you a different plan, give yourself time to experience the frustration and lack of fulfillment of the original idea. Talk to someone about your disappointment and frustration, then when you are ready, you can return to the project or experience and begin again or go on to something new. You may feel the need to begin again, even though it may be to continue the project with a new or expanded focus.

It will help you get through this disruptive period, if you are acknowledged for the frustration you are feeling, and then given appreciation for being willing to accept changes and begin again. Lack of acknowledgment and appreciation at a time like this can cause you to feel stuck or carry a grudge. Neither of these support your completing the idea or the project, which brings you joy and fulfillment.

One of the gifts of difficult times is the knowledge that you can endure and come out wiser and stronger on the other side. You can begin to trust your ability to handle change and still maintain order in your life, even if the plan did change. This will strengthen your confidence a lot, and make the next changes seem a little easier each time they happen.

Your strength as a Trunk carries the daily life force. When you are clear on the task and persevere, you will accomplish your deserved goal. When life is actualized in the third dimension, it must be supported and maintained by systems and structure, or life will be in continual chaos. In spite of our small pictures and concepts, there is a creative order and rhythm to the full orchestra of the universe. Your Trunk Point of Power supports life by maintaining order as part of your naturalness. This is a great blessing to all of us.

You are the steadfast energy of life, the solid people. The movement of human life depends on your stability, as the tree depends on the trunk. It is not your job to be responsible for the other Points of Power, just do your part like the trunk of the tree.

I worked with a couple who were experiencing distress in their relationship. They were also in business together, so the business was being affected too. When Jesse came to see me, he was feeling frustrated and angry with Sondra. He felt she was deliberately undermining his sense of accomplishment at work, and he wasn't going to stand for it any longer.

I asked him to describe what he felt was going on. He said his job in the company was production. He loved to gather the information, act as liaison with subcontractors and run the errands. His job was bringing the pieces together so he could complete his part of the project.

"Every time I have my list and I am ready to walk out the door," Jesse said, "Sondra comes up with one more idea about our product, and I am sick and tired of this! Why can't she plan ahead, and make up her mind, once and for all, so I can get on with my job?"

I asked Jesse if this happens often and how long had it been going on. He said, "This happens every day! Every day my plan is interrupted with one more idea from her. How are we ever going to meet the deadline? And not only that, even when she doesn't come up with one more idea, and I am in the warehouse working, she comes out and wants to "brainstorm" with me on the ten other projects she has running through her head. I can't take this much longer. This is affecting our personal life as well."

After asking Jesse a few more questions, it appeared to me that Jesse and Sondra were definitely on different frequencies. Sondra seemed to be a Leaf and Jesse was a strong Trunk Point of Power. He really tried to be patient and talk with Sondra, and yet what he really wanted to do was just do his project and not be interrupted.

Jesse and I spent some time talking about the Tree of Life. His eyes lit up. "You mean there is hope for us? We can really work this out, even though we are so-o-o different?" I assured him, all the possibilities are available for them, if they are equally committed to creating a bridge of communication between them.

We talked about his need to support his rhythm by working without interruption as much as possible, and his need to spend time on his project so they could meet their deadlines. It was also very important for Sondra to have someone to brainstorm with besides Jesse. This is her rhythm as a visionary and a big support for her creative movement.

I suggested they hire another person, even part time, so Sondra could have someone to share new ideas with and Jesse could have more production time. They hired Jackie, and Sondra began to direct more of her ideas and conversations to Jackie. The stress of so many interruptions was reduced and Jesse could actually feel excited about meeting the deadline, instead of feeling stressed.

"I'm so relieved," Jesse said. "You know, I really was feeling guilty about my impatience with Sondra's questions and ideas, and I didn't want to feel that way. I really love her creativity and curiosity. Since Jackie came on board, it sure is a relief for me. I can actually stay focused on my job in the company and Sondra really seems to enjoy her time with Jackie." Jesse and Sondra both learned the value of a Branch Point of Power in their life.

TRUNKS

FREQUENCY: Consistent Movement, logical progress in starting, creating, and completing projects or ideas.

SOUND: Water
Fluidity of movement within banks of human form
Body will experience bubbles of joy as life moves through orderly, strong, consistent patterns in life.

DESIRE: Have a plan or pattern for life
A beginning, middle, and completion
Support life to move with order, balance and harmony

GIFT: The Guardians of form in the world of our humanness
The part of us that is joyful to create and maintain order in the magic Kingdom of Earth.

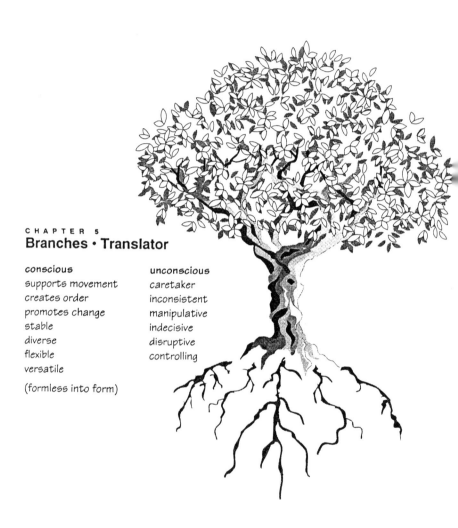

Branches • Translator

conscious	unconscious
supports movement	caretaker
creates order	inconsistent
promotes change	manipulative
stable	indecisive
diverse	disruptive
flexible	controlling
versatile	

(formless into form)

As you claim your Point of Power you can capture the energy of the unconscious attributes and refocus that power consciously.

Chapter 5

Branches

We live in a world of form. In order to become real, ideas (formless reality) must be materialized and brought into three-dimensional reality. Just as the branches on a tree connect the leaves with the trunk, so the Branch Point of Power connects ideas with form. Branches "Translate" the images and visions of the Leaves and accumulate the necessary resources (e.g. people, money, equipment and supplies) to accomplish their task and create a finished product or presentation. Branches' Point of Power is to connect with the Greater Vision and make it real in our everyday world.

Your motivation as a Branch is to gather the ideas, and create order with them into systems, formats and organizations. You bring the ideas to life for all of us to appreciate. Your naturalness is rewarded when you see your creation as a completed, functioning system.

You do not need guidelines for your project; you like to create your own guidelines and schedule. You are inspired by brainstorming ideas and then begin to shape these ideas into a reality we can all see and use. Branches are stimulated by ever-expanding possibilities in a project. You enjoy putting the pieces of the puzzle together and seeing the end result materialize. If the original idea changes as you go along, you easily adjust as long as you are accomplishing something and the goal is still in view.

One way your enthusiasm can be dampened is when the changes are given to you, rather than presented as options you can incorporate as you see fit. Branches are most creative when given full support to keep expanding a project, and do not feel hemmed in by someone else's ideas or limitations. You are usually quite open to change and expansion, as long as you can make the decision on how to use the expansions or changes.

Branches are valuable to our world. Life would be empty and stagnant without new ideas being delivered to us. This Point of Power is the glue, bringing the pieces together so life moves, works, has order in this dimension and supports our physical world. Fortunately, there seem to be more Branches and Trunks on this planet than any other frequencies. Since this is a world of form, we need many frequencies who naturally create the reality in which our Souls can participate.

When we give ourself permission to live and experience life from our natural frequency, our Point of Power, we feel comfortable and peaceful in our daily lives. Then we tend to express a lot more of our joy and love, because we are in our Essence, feeling less stressed. Our sound of Life is heard clearly.

Branches who live from their Point of Power can truly look like lucky or blessed people. They seem to be able to flow through life, adjust, create and have fun. Their versatility and adaptability is a great sponsor of flow and balancing change in life.

Employment options are plentiful and varied because of your flexibility with life and your motivation to create change. Your services are in demand, because you are so naturally good at this translation called, organizing.

You may change employment often because of your desire to work with new projects regularly. In reviewing a resume on the life of a Branch, you may have a long job history and many varied experiences. You may have been told that you are irresponsible, unable to commit to people or projects or haven't settled down yet. What is really happening is that Branches are naturally part of the "start up" in life or on a project. That is your joy and enthusiasm, to be on the ground floor and get things going. Once things are going (usually about two to two-and-a-half-years), and life or the project has become pretty routine, your antenna will be open to receiving new areas in life for you to deliver your creativity.

If the present experience or project continues to open up new areas of creativity for you, new beginnings, you will not feel the need to change jobs or relationships. You can continue to expand and deliver your gifts in life, right where you are. As a matter of fact, most of the time you prefer staying where you are. You move on only when you know you aren't free to create and deliver your enthusiasm for life, because the project no longer calls for that, or the relationship isn't supporting your need to be a part of new beginnings.

All of us have a desire to do something new or different at times. For Branches, that's a natural part of your motivation for living and creating. A Branch is stimulated and excited about a new project. You may have several degrees, a varied employment background, and many travel experiences from following your Point of Power. It's your naturalness.

You may also find yourself involved as a counselor, a good listener or a mediator, because your role is that of a Translator. Many situations in life require some translation, so relating can be clearer and for communication and cooperation to be effective. You are quite good in these situations, because this is just another place to put the pieces of the puzzle together in another way. These pieces sometimes make the difference in the success or dissolution of a project or relationship.

My client Gary said to me, "You know, Kay, I don't know what's wrong with me. I get so excited about my work and seem to be interested for awhile, until my enthusiasm drains away and I feel like a balloon with a slow leak. I want to change this, but I don't know how or where to begin, or even if I can. I get a lot of flack about not staying committed to what I'm doing. I try to change the way I'm looking at my work and revive my enthusiasm, and I just can't seem to get going again."

Gary and I did the visualization and I explained the different frequencies, using the analogy of the Tree of Life. Gary's Point of Power is clearly a Branch. When I explained about the Branches of the tree and their relationship with the Leaves and Trunk, Gary got a big grin on his face.

"Wow! What I'm doing is okay, isn't it? There's really nothing wrong with me. I am so relieved. This is a natural way for me to live, and all these years, I thought I was doing something wrong. Enough people sure told me I was."

Gary and I have had a few conversations since this session, and he told me he received a promotion to department head for a new division in the company. He was thrilled, because he was in a restless stage when we did our session. He reported that things have changed in his relationship of two years. Cheryl seems a lot more exciting and adventuresome now.

The point is this, any time we take the judgment off ourselves and give ourselves permission to be natural and powerful, who we really are, our whole world seems to change too. This is the way we co-create. We change our view of Life, and Life reflects back a new picture. Because we see and feel differently inside, we create and attract Life in a new way.

BRANCHES

FREQUENCY: Flexible movement, able to adapt to many paces and many places and use the changes as spark for creativity.

SOUND: Fire
Spark of creation/transformation
Body registers excitement at the prospect of new ideas, new projects, new people, new experiences

DESIRE: Watch creation take place before their eyes
Take the unseen ideas and give them life in form

GIFT: Express our Divine Humanness by bringing Spirit into form.
The part of us that loves to put the pieces of life together and see them work.

CHAPTER 6
Leaves • Visionary

conscious	unconscious
ideas	unrealistic
concepts	evasive
vision	judgmental
initiation	disassociated
challenge	impractical
movement	impatient
(formless)	

As you claim your Point of Power you can capture the energy of the unconscious attributes and refocus that power consciously.

Chapter 6

Leaves

J ust as there are many more Leaves on a tree than Branches, the
Trunk or the Roots, so we will have many more words to describe
this frequency. The Visionary part of us is our link, a doorway to
our Soul, through our mind, and in most lives, it's an unfamiliar
doorway. Since there are many visions, there are many doorways
for each of us to access the wisdom and vision of our Souls. Leaves
of a tree are constantly involved with movement from a variety of
sources, and the kind of mind identified with Leaves is constantly
involved with ideas and creation, stimulated from all sources in
life. Leaves are a receiving station for ideas and inventions in our
lives. Theirs is the world of the formless, the abstract.

Leaves Point of Power is the ability to create in concept,
and see the larger vision of Life, stimulating and inspiring those
around to greater action. In expressing your Point of Power you
are driven by the motivation to continually create and recreate.
When you complete a project, if you do, it feels like the end,
like death. And yet you experience a great sense of joy to see
your ideas born. What is easiest for you, is to have the process
be heavily supported by the Branches and Trunks. Then it feels
wonderful and fulfilling.

Your reward is movement and the sense of freedom. Even
though a lot of your action is created inside your mind, you still
experience the freedom of movement. When you hear an idea, you
immediately piggy-back on that, springboarding to other ideas,
some associated, some not. Leaves can never implement all the

ideas you receive. Living and delivering in the three-dimensional world of implementation is not your Point of Power.

Freedom for you is learning to live in this dimension and using your creativity to design your life so you can support your naturalness, while allowing movement of your visionary mind. This sense of freedom increases your self-esteem, when you can do some regular things, feel good about them and not feel trapped.

Your mind moves so rapidly that it often involves physical action, too. A natural expression for Leaves is to be talking, walking around, and playing with something in your hands at the same time. Physical movement helps reduce the pressure of constantly receiving ideas. In most cases, Leaves find it VERY DIFFICULT to sit still, for a long time, and not talk, or draw, or doodle. Since this is a requirement in our school systems, most schools are not designed to support our visionary children. An example of this is Thomas Edison, who was purportedly sent home from first grade with a note from his teacher: "This child is uneducatable." History indicates he was a visionary child.

I feel it is essential that we create alternative methods of education for the Leaves children, so the natural movement of their frequency can be expressed and supported. Then others around them can celebrate their creativity, not confine it.

Because followthrough and implementation are not a strength for Leaves, support from Branches (the translators of formless into form) is a tremendous relief. These relationships provide someone to talk with who can relate to the visionary consciousness, and offer guidelines on how to say it, do it, or deliver it in life. This validation helps overcome the criticism from many who judge Leaves as too idealistic, airy-fairy, ungrounded and irresponsible.

Without support from the rest of the Tree of Life, you doubt your own vision, your own Point of Power. You try to speak or act another way, so you can be accepted and feel loved and understood. Nevertheless we cannot have Leaves on a tree, without Roots, Trunk and Branches.

To imprison the Visionary Self, to gain approval, always brings disease and stress into our lives. You can not sell out your Soul and live in peace. You must allow your naturalness, your Point of Power, your Light, to fully shine, no matter how you are perceived by others. If your intention is to deliver your Point of Power from the highest, clearest place (Leaves), you don't bring harm to the rest of the tree. You are being responsible for your part of the Tree of Life. It may not bring approval or understanding for you, but it is your mode as a Soul. You came into the Earth to be a Leaf and actively participate with the Greater Vision, to receive new visions and bring them into the earth plane.

New visions and new ideas threaten old visions and old ideas, no matter where they come from. We are here to change and yet we resist change. Therefore, approval and understanding are not the common responses a Visionary receives. You strengthen your capacity to demonstrate a clear vision, when you trust who you are, and reach agreement with your Soul and the Earth.

Honor your agreement with your Soul, and agree to fully live your frequency. Then you can reduce the feeling of separation and judgment from the rest of the tree—Branches, Trunk or Roots. Each part of the Tree of Life has a view of reality very different from the Leaves' view. Each individual sees life from their Point of Power, not from yours. It's the only way we can be, until we learn there are views other than ours.

Everyone has a doorway to their Greater Vision. From my experience, there is a much smaller group of Souls who choose to have a Leaf frequency as their Point of Power. This again increases the possibility of not being understood by the greater number of Branches or Trunks. They don't have as many opportunities to relate to and get to know how Leaves function. Lack of under-standing is a breeding ground for judgment and blame.

Since this is a world of form, we need lots of people whose fre-quency is Roots, Trunk or Branches. We do not need to have a lot of persons whose frequency is Leaves, because each one receives more ideas than they, as an individual, can ever implement. Thus, as the Leaves drop, they are here to bring, "drop," new ideas into our three-dimensional world, to be absorbed into the Roots, feed-ing into the Trunk and Branches. Then Branches translate the ideas into form/projects and pass them on to the Trunk, to be maintained and then connected with the Roots, so the life of the idea/project/experience can be sustained in this Earth. This is Divine Teamwork!

Self-confidence is often lacking in these creative individuals because they see social behavior in others that they can't match or understand. This creates self-doubt or a "one-down" feeling. It's a major constriction for Leaves to try to perform according to others' beliefs and behaviors. Because Leaves live in such a conceptual reality, it's often difficult for them to translate into words what their minds experience. They feel misunderstood, and often are, since there's a loss of communication between them and others.

When talking with Leaves, you may notice a blank look in their eyes, but they have not abandoned you or shut you off. They are creating their own movie inspired from the ideas you're sharing. They will return to you, probably several miles down the road of thought. And when your communication begins again, it may seem confused or unclear. You see, they "completed" the process in their minds, and rejoined your conversation, having missed a whole segment of what you were talking about.

If you are a Branch, Trunk or Root person you may notice missing pieces of information when communicating with Leaves. This is a common experience in conversation with a Leaf, because the Leaf mind moves so quickly, in so many directions, at the same time. Sometimes the Leaf is giving you information from several places of consciousness. If the conversation has holes in it, touch the Leaf (this helps provide some grounding) and say, "I'm not sure I understand. Could you give me some more details or information?" Keep asking questions until the holes are filled in for you. The Leaf does not recognize these missing pieces you are experiencing.

Leaves may also display impatience with your questions, because their minds have to slow down and backtrack for a moment, when they are used to a pace of "fast forward." If your questions are truly for more information and greater understanding of the Leaf's ideas, they can usually pause and give you more details, unless they are in a vision frequency at the moment and need to complete that cycle.

Because their ideas are so often invalidated, Leaves may lack confidence in their own Point of Power. They have learned to defend their ideas and freedom of creativity. What they truly want is to share these ideas, so your persistence will pay off for both of you. It's not from a superior point of view, being secretive or manipulative that they communicate this way, it's their natural way to create and recreate conceptually. Most of the time, they're not aware of the missing pieces. The key to communicating with a Leaf is to support the focus of the conversation with questions, to fill in the missing pieces. Because they create and recreate in thought, they also do this in starting sentences. They may start and start and start again, rarely completing a sentence, just starting new ones.

How we view life from our Point of Power determines how we experience other people in our lives. When we accept our Point of Power, we allow more space in our lives for others to express their Points of Power.

For example, several years ago, Ray, nineteen years old, attended a weekend seminar I conducted. He was an abused child who never felt safe. His family ridiculed and harassed him for the way he talked. They said, "You're crazy to think that way," "You are such a chicken!" Ray grew up living in fear, whether he was at home or in school. No one understood him, including himself, and he was always being chased and beaten up on the way to and from school.

When I met Ray, I hadn't yet received any information about Point of Power. As I experienced more and more about our Points of Power, I shared it with Ray. I remember the day I shared some insight with him about Leaves, and he looked at me, with tears in his eyes, and said, "You mean I'm okay? I'm not crazy like they said?"

"Ray," I said, "you are more than okay. You have a magical mind that creates in a unique way. Not everyone's mind thinks in the way yours does. You are absolutely okay!" As I have been given more insights and experience, over the years, I have shared this with Ray. He has used this tool to assess his life in a new way and this has helped restore his sense of self-worth and self-love.

Many Leaves, in order to survive, learn to use their frequency to get approval through their accomplishments. Since this is a world of form, the Trunk and the Branches have frequencies that, many times, are easier to relate to, and it is easier for them to accomplish Earthly tasks.

Some Leaves I've known have used their creative, rapid minds to mimic the behavior of Trunks and Branches, in order to work a "regular" job and get paid money. These skills, absorbed by a Leaf, are valuable to support human daily needs, while learning to trust their own Point of Power as a Visionary.

The Leaves' greatest challenge arises after they have learned to function in life as a Trunk or a Branch. When they change to transmit their frequency on their own Point of Power, they are unfamiliar with their true frequency/rhythm. Tuning into their own frequency can seem like an identity crisis, until the Leaves become familiar and trusting of their true Soul sound of life.

Having support from others who accept, love and recognize your naturalness, your Point of Power, helps this transition feel much safer. The Branches provide a connection for the Leaves with the rest of the Tree of Life; these relationships are usually fulfilling for both.

We all—Roots, Trunk, Branches and Leaves—can access our Souls, our Greater Vision, if we choose to. Each frequency from the Tree of Life may have a different doorway to the Greater Vision, and each path is always the perfect way for each person and their Point of Power. The more you know and accept your naturalness, the easier it is to journey with your Soul.

Since we have explored the Tree of Life, I hope you'll begin to have an awareness of the untapped power available to you, as you remember who you are, release your limited beliefs and behaviors and shine from your naturalness, your Point of Power. By understanding and accepting your Point of Power and gaining a new awareness of the realities of others, you can create a more peaceful, loving, harmonious world. When you give yourself permission to sing your natural song and dance your spontaneous dance, life works, and we all win!

The child in each of us is screaming to love and be loved, and to have the freedom to create. Now is the time!

ADDITIONAL INFORMATION ON LEAVES

Life Spin

There is an experience I have watched Leaves go through that I would like to share with you. This experience may have happened to you as a visionary or when you happened to be in the Leaves as your modality for the moment. I have called this experience a Life Spin. It looks and feels like this: You are going through your life and everything seems to be pretty normal; something happens in your day that sends you into a spin. You can feel the acceleration of your mind and feelings, everything seems to be whirling so fast you find it difficult to think. You may begin to feel dizzy at the rate your emotions are moving through you. The mind and feelings seem to have lost their ability to communicate or work together. Overload takes over! Any feelings or thoughts you have will feel and look overwhelming at this time. This experience is like dropping into an abyss or going through a dark tunnel that seems to have no doors or windows, nor other choices or options you can see or recognize at this time.

As a Leaf, you have the ability to see the bigger picture naturally. This is an asset. If your mind sees the bigger picture through the eyes of fear, your emotions get enrolled, and the Life Spin begins. At this moment, the bigger picture becomes a liability because with fear as the lens—how you view this situation in your life—the picture will continue to expand and the fear will increase and feel overwhelming. The Leaf part of you always sees life in the biggest possible way and when your emotions get involved in the picture, the power is provided to activate these visions. If fear is the emotion involved, that is the feeling that gets activated with this vision, you can feel frozen in your movement by fear. Constant or rapid movement is the life force for a Leaf so when a Leaf feels frozen, a sense of desperation, feeling trapped, or feeling suffocated may occur.

A Life Spin usually occurs as we move through our life to the next level of our vision, so we are usually breaking down some limiting beliefs and allowing our mind and emotions to embrace new beliefs and new feelings. Even though this experience is uncomfortable and frightening, it usually preceeds a major breakthrough. When you are in this experience, one of the ways to support yourself to move through the darkness to the light is to ask for support. Call a friend, someone you trust and who knows you well, and will be willing to listen to you from an unconditionally loving place. Ask this friend to listen to you and to give you guidance and reflections on your process. Questions from your friend are essential for this intense experience, even if you don't answer the questions. They provide a way to change your frozen focus, begin to feel movement again and make new choices to support getting through the Life Spin.

This is one of the times that outside information from another person is very important to open up doors and windows for your movement. You may not use any of the advice or guidance given, so it is also important that your friend does not have an attachment to your using their advice. The important thing is that as your friend speaks to you, the spin will begin to feel differently and your mind will begin to explore this experience from a different view, as options are presented to help you return to a place of balance with your mind and emotions. This may happen in the first five minutes of conversation or take a few hours, and it will occur.

LEAVES

FREQUENCY: Fast, continuous movement (words, body, mind— sometimes all three)

SOUND: Air
Breath in the body
Body experiences the sense of freedom, flight, no limits
Can go anywhere, do anything

DESIRE: Freedom to follow their own imagination
Freedom of expression and movement in life

GIFT: Our connection with our Divine Child within through our innocence and joy of life.
The part of us that believes anything is possible!

Chapter 7

Communication

Communication is your right to hear and be heard. Communication is not about agreement. Communication creates a bridge that allows you to enter another's reality and explore how their world looks and feels to them. Then you can examine how you can relate to their world exchange ideas and stories and explore life together. Communicating with each other is like trying on new clothes. Sometimes you have to try on several outfits, go to several stores, before you find something that fits. Communication is a dance of verbal exchange with another person to facilitate discovery and intimacy at new levels. Clear communication supports opening avenues for truth to be exchanged and for you to experience acknowledgment, acceptance and appreciation with or without agreement.

When you recognize and accept your Point of Power, an amazing thing happens. You begin to see people, relationships and interactions in your life from a new vantage point. You have less need for others to behave like you, think like you, believe like you and live their daily lives like you. You no longer need to be validated by others' choices, behaviors and beliefs. Communication becomes an adult-to-adult experience.

I feel safe hearing you, even if your ideas and feelings are different than my expression or experience of the very same thing, I can learn about another way to look at life through your reality. By recognizing and accepting my Point of Power, I accept that your

59

Point of Power may be different than mine, and I am not threatened by our uniqueness.

When you begin to accept another as they are, rather than as you think they should be, this is a primary step necessary for creating any fulfilling relationship.

By letting go of the need for agreement in communication and allowing it to be an expression of your mutual experience from different vantage points, you can dramatically reduce your levels of judgment and criticism of others. You have opened a major door to love, called acceptance, and are beginning to remove yourself from the narrow tunnel called right or wrong. The tunnel of judgment that houses right and wrong *never* allows acceptance to be the resolution or any situation to be win/win. You are trapped by blame: someone has to be wrong! When you release the need to be in judgment of others, you have begun to be committed to an intimate relationship with love and your soul.

Whatever judgment or criticism you have of others, you have first judged and criticized yourself, and then passed it on.

To release yourself from the tunnel of judgment, the first step is to accept yourself just as you are now, your life and the choices you made to bring you to this time in your life. Accepting yourself is a rebirth for your soul. This allows you to assess all the resources you have accumulated throughout your life and make new choices that will begin to create life as you want to experience it now. When you accept yourself, acceptance of another is natural and joyful. This opens the door for you to love and be loved. Acceptance is the breath of freedom. Joy is a natural result of acceptance. Joy gives birth to creativity, the expression of the Divine Child within.

When your Divine Child within is turned loose to create, the first thing you want is playmates, someone to share the joy of living with. Self-acceptance increases your possibilities of finding someone who wants to play with you. If you like yourself, it makes it a lot easier for someone else to like you. Sometimes some relationships just seem to be easier to create and some relationships feel harder or not as much fun. Let's explore how your Point of Power may influence your relationships with others.

Relationships between the Roots and Trunk usually have a common avenue of understanding based on their connection with the concrete and solid parts of life, their appreciation of consistency in life. The Trunk and Branches work well together as teammates, like a bowl and the fruit in the bowl. The Trunk provides the systems and the Branches brings in the activity to add to the systems. The Branches and the Leaves like to play in the Universe, catch the falling stars of ideas and weave them into everyday life. They want to make the dreams come true today.

There is a natural dance between these Points of Power. The frequencies mesh, the movement in relationships and communication is natural and easy. These are relationships that seem to just happen, fit together, and flow easily. It's a wonderful gift to have relationships in your life that feel comfortable and compatible.

If there is stress in these relationships, it's from our personality distortions and the behavior we create with each other as a result of our patterning throughout our life. In seeking compatibility, because the Points of Power here are natural bridges, you have a good, solid foundation to build a strong, healthy relationship by letting go of the distortions.

The art of communication is accepting yourself and others, and practicing until the desired result is obtained. It helps to be willing to see and hear with bigger eyes and ears.

We are designed with one mouth and two ears. Good communication needs to follow these natural guidelines: listen twice as much as we talk!

There are some Point of Power combinations that require a conscious bridge of communication to be built and maintained. These relationships may feel like they take more effort to have things run smoothly. Knowing this, you can consciously invest energy in these relationships and make choices with greater clarity so the experiences create a win/win for both partners. The following combinations require a conscious commitment to bridge communication through love, respect, and cooperation, and a true desire to hear each other.

Leaves and Trunk   (Chapter 8)

Branches and Roots   (Chapter 9)

Leaves and Roots   (Chapter 10)

You can see by these combinations there are pieces of the tree missing. Leaves are connected to the trunk through branches. Branches are connected to the roots through a trunk. Just as these combinations are not the natural way a tree grows and lives, so it is in relationships. With these Points of Power there are some natural rhythms missing that can consciously be created to bridge the communication gaps. The gaps between the Points of Power are where communication breaks down and judgment enters, allowing our distortions to be projected onto another's reality. This can result in the lose/lose syndrome, or the right and wrong game or making your partner your enemy, rather than your teammate. Any one of these behaviors will severely weaken your relationship foundation. All you need to know is what is missing and how to fill it in. Then you can feel courageous and strong to make changes in your relationship by making different choices in your life.

There are no missing pieces in any Divine plan, no matter how it looks and feels to us from our human view of life. Releasing our distortions seems to be a lifetime process. There are as many ways to explore our distortions as there are people who have them.

TIPS ON INTERRELATIONSHIPS

Leaves and Branches

Branches and Trunk

Trunk and Roots

These three combinations of Points of Power live side by side on the Tree of Life, and they share a common connection to each other so they can usually communicate easily, unless they are dealing with personality issues.

Leaves use words as "fuel" for their movement. They constantly piggy-back or springboard off words to create their pictures and process. The key in communicating with Leaves is to have as much room as possible in the conversation to include their mental exploration and words they want to share with you about their visionary journey. This means you will probably have to hold the focus of the conversation and ask questions if it feels like some pieces of information are missing.

Branches use words for exploring, connecting and translating their reality. They put the pieces of vision and reality together for new creations. They gather ideas, data, techniques, processes and systems as part of their tools of creation. They love to assemble all the pieces and then create something new. They are open to ideas about their project/process and they do not like to be told how to create.

Trunks want words to create a step-by-step method, to provide information or missing pieces, to give them direction in their movement or project and to support consistency in their lives. Acquiring full details of the steps needed to complete a project is very important for the Trunks. They want all the information, *before beginning*, and then they want to be undisturbed or not have the plan altered *until* they complete it.

Roots use words like fertilizer. No matter how many words are poured out in their direction, they only take in what supports their reality. They have little interest in a lot of words about anything, particularly about conceptual subjects. They receive communication through the senses, and words feel like static to their nervous system. They can receive only a limited amount of words before they feel frustrated or distressed.

Leaves and Branches

These two Points of Power are natural partners. They live right next door to each other on the Tree of Life and are very supportive of each other. The thing they have in common is their joy of participating with formless reality. This is the natural place a Leaf lives and receives ideas from, many more than they know what to do with. The Branch provides a partner for implementation, a point of reference on what is really possible to accomplish here in the world of form and how long it might take.

Because the Leaves feel heard and supported by the Branches, who understand their rhythm, they are more trusting of suggestions for change or implementation. Trust is a key foundational ingredient in establishing all relationships, regardless of the Point of Power. Communication here can become almost intuitive when they really are brainstorming on the same wave length. They truly spark each other to greater possibilities.

Branches are motivated by new ideas that generate new beginnings, so they are inspired by their time spent with Leaves. Leaves are grateful to have someone to talk with about all these ideas, someone who can give them possibilities for realizing some of the ideas. Most important, Leaves do not have to do the creation by themselves.

Both Points of Power have a similar rhythm in movement so they can spontaneously create changes, still feel safe with each other and have fun being flexible together. This combination feeds off each other's creativity, just as fire and air feed off each other, so they are a powerful team to generate change. They want to make these changes now. Patience may not be a virtue of these teammates and continuous creativity is. They have a lot of fun together.

Branches and Trunks

This combination works well together because they like to see an end result from their efforts. Branches like to bring the ideas into form and the Trunks like to organize, coordinate and monitor the form. If the Branches are in a brainstorming mode, this can be challenging for the Trunks, because they like to receive the plan without numerous changes and then implement it. Timing is an important feature here. If the Branches bring their ideas to the Trunks too soon, before there really is a plan to be used, the Trunks can feel frustrated, if they feel they are responsible for doing something that is not clearly defined.

Trunk people really like to create from beginning to end and not be interrupted or have the original plan be altered, especially without their input. So the most workable, amicable and efficient team between the Branches and Trunks is when the plan is in place. Then the Branches know what they want, clearly communicate the plan and procedure to the Trunks and then just cheer them on with no more ideas and changes at that time.

Since we live in a world of form, this combination is very powerful in providing support and changes that assist our daily lives, through consistency and reliability. Imagine what it would be like if nothing happened when you dialed the phone, the grocery store was only open when the clerks felt like it, everyone drove on the side of the street they wanted to, no one collected the garbage, the bus driver never used the same route or a schedule or you never knew when you would receive your pay check.

The systems generated and maintained by the Branches and Trunks are a contributing factor to our daily sense of safety and balance. This is dramatically demonstrated when there is a loss of our most basic systems—water, electricity, roads, stores, gas stations, banks—through a disaster. Without these systems supporting the order and rhythm necessary in cities and populated areas, chaos can result and fear can escalate rapidly. Consistency helps our body, mind and emotions feel much safer and able to cope with life.

This combination is a powerful team for accomplishment. When they come together with a common focus and freedom to generate the results they want, the end results are quite amazing and satisifying for everyone, a real sense of fulfillment.

Trunks and Roots

Have you heard the phrase, "salt of the earth"? This duo truly represents that expression, by being very practical, real, down to earth and with a just-get-the-job-done attitude. This team's power is in form. They live, move and create in form and feel safe doing that. They feel best when they can follow a rhythm that is congruent with the earth's rhythm. Even their sleep patterns may be closely associated to the day and night schedules.

This combination will focus on simple, basic ways to live, to accomplish the task, to organize, to regenerate, to relate. This is truly living life without the frills, just as it is. There is a real strength and stability coming from this foundational acceptance of life. This is the power that had to be present in the pioneers who came across the United States, persevering, one day at a time, meeting life as it was presented to them. Stability and simplicity provide balance in life.

Leaves and Roots

This relationship can be used as a point of balance for the Leaf person. Because the Leaves live in concept and vision, there are times that their reality feels unsafe and they need to be grounded and feel centered. An evening or an afternoon with a Root person is such a blessing for a Leaf in these moments. Because the Roots live in a solid and tangible reality, as real, earthy people, they provide a good reference point for the Leaves to re-establish their focus and movement from.

Roots have a natural sense of life, so they access "vision," in another way, and they have this in common with the Leaves. The Roots usually *feel* the vision more than *see* it. An afternoon or evening with a Leaf is usually inspiring and fulfills any curiosity Roots may have about vision seen through another's eyes. Roots people are usually open to new experiences that allow them to participate, at their own rhythm, and not have to talk a lot.

It is natural for Leaves to talk a lot because they have so many ideas always going through their minds. Since Roots don't like to talk much, they are a good audience for the Leaf. The biggest stretch for both of these Points of Power to spend much time together comes through the significant difference in their rhythm with life. Roots are slow and deep. Leaves are fast and moving.

If their time together is informal and a grounding experience for the Leaf and a sharing time for the Roots, this interaction can be natural and easy. The challenge is when there is a deadline to meet and details to work with that require communication and cooperation.

Remember, when the Leaf sees a vision, it is done, the picture is complete for them. They expect life to produce the results just as quickly as they saw it. This is not how life is in this dimension. The timing for manifestation is different here than in our vision world. The Leaf will want the results now, and the Roots will know the natural rhythm of creating in an everyday world.

In order to work together, each Point of Power will need to have patience with the other, listen carefully and communicate fully, until the two realities have a common foundation to work from. This foundation will probably fit into the Trunk Point of Power by the time they are through. Creating a plan, having a goal for completion and the steps to get there that work for both parties will help reduce stress and frustration as the project proceeds.

Because the rhythms are so different, this provides a nice break from the ordinary routine of life and relationships, and can be quite an enriching and practical experience for both people.

Leaves and Trunks

This combination will have similarities to the Leaves and Roots. The difference is the Trunk is more consciously committed to details, order and a plan. Where Roots sense the rhythm in life, the Trunk creates and maintains order and the systems. The Trunk Point of Powers, in order to feel secure in movement, will want the interaction with the Leaf to be well defined, whether this is an informal situation or a business project. In an informal or social setting, as a rule, Trunks will require fewer details than they want in a business situation. The amount of detail here will be based on their confidence in the social setting.

If the interaction is a business situation, where a goal is to be met and a plan enacted, the Trunk will want very clear details written down: dates, resources needed, location, and so on. Requests for this much information, from a Leaf, are usually quite frustrating, because in their world, the project is done. "Why would you want all this information?" The Leaves create and create and continue creating. Once the vision is complete in their mind they have no passion to go over it again and again, and answering a lot of questions feels redundant to them. And yet, this is absolutely necessary if the Trunk is to feel clear and proceed with confidence with the plan.

So, can you see, the number one ingredient here is respect, followed by patience. Each Point of Power must respect the other's rhythm of movement. The Leaf *must* slow down and answer questions until all the necessary details are given so the Trunk can proceed. The Trunk must feel safe enough to keep asking all the questions necessary to fill in the details, so as to begin the project with confidence and enthusiasm.

The strain in their interaction will come if the Leaf gives too few details, and then keeps changing the plan and interrupting the Trunk after they have begun the project. The main reason Trunks want all the details at the beginning of the project is they do not like their progress to be interrupted by a change of plans in the middle of their creation. They like to have a plan, and to complete the plan on time.

Since life is about change, all the time, this relationship is set up to be frustrating to both parties unless there is a strong commitment to respect, understand and appreciate each other and the value each is to the other. The missing piece of the Tree of Life is the Branches, so the Leaf and Trunk must create their own bridge, and translate these two realities by stretching to accommodate the other person's needs.

These relationships are really worth cultivating and sustaining. They provide great resources for each other and wonderful opportunity to expand possibilities and include a new way to look at life. These are not the relationships that "just happen," they truly require a good solid love base, a conscious commitment to grow together and perseverance to learn new ways of seeing, thinking, and acting out life with each other. Each person can experience a great sense of accomplishment by working together in relationships of this combination.

I find many combinations like this in business and personal relationships. When people discover it is "normal" to have these feelings of confusion and distress with each other, and still want to work or live together, they are quite relieved to discover a very conscious way to accomplish that. I have seen some really solid, powerful relationships develop through this combination. I think this is probably the most challenging combination because their visions of life are so different and so are their rhythms. Yet a Leaf who feels understood and supported by a Trunk knows loyalty at its best. A Trunk who feels safe and appreciated by a Leaf really feels valuable and acknowledged.

Branches and Roots

Branches are the Translators. They have great affinity with the abstract and the formless, and they love creating with form. Since this is their natural rhythm, even though they are separated from the Roots by the Trunk, they can easily make that transition and share time with the Roots. They simultaneously feel a sense of their own Point of Power, and an understanding of the Roots and the world they live in.

Inspired by new possibilities, Branches are eager to receive new ideas and explore ways to incorporate these ideas into their reality or their project. They rarely feel intruded upon by others sharing ideas with them, unless that individual wants to control or limit them or their project. Then they are closed to the person and the idea. The more ideas that come to them, through themselves or others, the more excitement they feel. They love putting the pieces of the puzzle together. This is especially true if they are given freedom to assemble the resources necessary to get the project off the ground, and guide the development according to their pace and vision.

Since the Roots are so foundational—solid and reliable—it is usually easy for the Branches to access this support and know when and where to use it. The caution here is for the Branches to monitor their high level of enthusiasm and movement to allow and include the rhythm of the Roots, in order to receive the gifts the Roots offer to any project or relationships. The Roots will deliver their gifts if the space is made available for them. Otherwise, they will not market their skills and abilities to be included in a program, project or a relationship. They are very loyal and enduring in their connections with people.

If this relationship between a Branch and a Root were to be a long-term, daily experience, they would definitely need to create guidelines for their communication to flow easily and to satisfy the needs they each have for their natural rhythm. With commitment and willingness from both people, it is really quite workable and most of the time easily maintained. It does require conscious recognition of the needs of each other and clarification of the desired results. This is a valuable connection for both partners and can be quite refreshing to share in each other's world.

Chapter 8

How Do Leaves and Trunks Communicate?

This combination will have similarities to the Leaves and Roots. The difference is the Trunk is more consciously committed to details, order and a plan. Where Roots sense the rhythm in life, the Trunks create and maintain order and the systems. Trunk people, in order to feel secure in their movement, will want the interaction between them and the Leaf to be well defined, whether this is an informal situation or a business project.

This is a challenging bridge to create. The Leaves and Trunks have a totally different relationship with form. The Leaves are concerned with movement, creating and recreating. Trunks want to participate in life through order and consistency, to know what's happening as much as possible, the solid and reliable side of life.

The Leaf views life as a visionary. The Trunk views life as a maintainer. Each of these expressions of creativity is essential to life. Yet there is little or no conscious appreciation of the other's view of life. Sometimes there is a lot of criticism and judgment of each other, filled with expectation. "You should be different than you are, then I wouldn't be so stressed."

Some Trunks use this relationship as a subtle way to avoid recognizing and claiming their own Point of Power, by deferring their power to the Leaf expression of creativity, as the only valuable way to create. This is not true. It may be a more visible expression, and that does not make it more valuable. Uniqueness is not confined or assigned to a few. We are all unique. Appreciation of our uniqueness is activated by our acceptance of who we are. Our acceptance of who we are increases our uniqueness. This is a powerful exchange, and helps us discover our natural rhythm in our daily life.

This is a three-dimensional world, and if you've come into it with your Point of Power as a Trunk, and you'd rather be a Leaf, you are denying the value of your naturalness and strength. Form must be created and maintained. This sustains our bodies and lives.

As a Trunk Point of Power your movement and creation will rarely look like that of a Leaf who creates in concept and expects three-dimensional life to move at the same pace. Concept moves much faster than form; it is, after all, formless. The Trunk energy supports life in the third dimension, and moves at the pace of this dimension which is slower than concept, not less valuable.

Leaves tend to envy the seemingly simple lives of the Trunk people who:

1. Make a decision and follow it through.

2. Know how to create order.

3. Know what they want and go for it.

4. Are reliable, i.e. show up on time, keep commitments etc.

Or the Leaves may resent Trunk people, feeling that they:

1. Are inflexible and don't want to change.

2. "Never understand" the Leaves and their ideas.

3. Always want things done their way.

4. Are too slow, take too long to get anything done.

Do you see how these are two sides of the same coin? It depends on how we choose to view another's reality, either as valuable or negate their value.

Since Leaves create in concept, they continually experience three-dimensional life as too slow and may blame it on others' inefficiency. Efficiency has nothing to do with it. The problem is two different rhythms of creativity—one formless and one of form. Many times, watching a Leaf and Trunk relate, it looks like they both showed up at the same dance, and each one hears and dances to different music, reflecting their own natural rhythms.

If you're involved in a Leaf/Trunk relationship of any kind, begin to listen to how you blame each other. What we blame another for is usually our own vulnerability experiencing fear of loss, somewhere in our life. You'll learn a lot about your expectations of yourself and about your behavior, as you begin to listen to your own inner and outer dialogue with your partner. The other person doesn't have to be wrong in order for you to be okay.

How can a bridge be created between the Leaf and the Trunk? Is it possible? I believe anything is possible when we discover options that are available and consciously choose intimacy and cooperation, rather than choosing conditions of separation. In viewing the tree, the leaves are connected to the trunk through branches. So it is in this relationship, there must be Branches built, through communication, so each person can access the other's reality. This bridge will not build itself; once built, it must be consciously maintained. This means the Leaf must slow down and *listen* to the Trunk's words about his or her feelings, thoughts or experiences. Maybe it is true the Leaf can see something different than the Trunk sees. This view of another's reality must always be presented as "another view," not a replacement for what the Trunk is experiencing from their own reality and feelings.

Trunk people must S T R E T C H their views and systematic approach to life to a greater point of flexibility and spontaneity in order to embrace the view of the Leaves. Patience is required to allow the Leaves to share their view, and all the versions they can see possible, for any one situation, and support the Leaves to stay focused on the original goal of the conversation. Any place in the conversation you do not understand what the Leaf is talking about, the Trunk must ask questions. The Leaf cannot know what pieces are missing in the conversation if the Trunk doesn't ask.

The key to maintaining the bridge is to respect the differences in your realities and be excited to explore the expanded world you can discover together by entering each other's reality through reverence and communication. To have an easy flow in this relationship will require practice, patience with yourself and each other, love and appreciation. Each partner must work at this relationship to create and maintain a win/win.

These relationships are really worth cultivating and sustaining. They provide great resources for each partner and a wonderful opportunity to expand possibilities and include a new way to look at life. Each person can experience a great sense of accomplishment by working together in relationships of this combination.

PERSONAL RELATIONSHIPS

Let's begin to look at the Leaf/Trunk personal relationship. I see this combination often in personal, business and family relationships. The challenge of this requires the awakening and growth of everyone involved, regardless of how comfortable it may feel. Comfort is not always an indicator that the situation is healthy. A Leaf can lose touch with details and information necessary to create order in daily life. The questions a Trunk asks to receive guidelines, can help ground the Leaf in the practical side of life as well as the vision.

A Trunk may become rigid and routine in thinking and behavior. After all, comfort is consistency. The continuous movement of a Leaf offers the Trunk the opportunity to see other options are available for all situations in life, and expand his or her experience beyond the comfort zone.

We seek in others what is missing in ourselves. There's a strong initial attraction between these two rhythms, and that can be exciting and interesting, and it may also create resistance, rejection, denial and blame. Magnets attract or repel. The purpose of this connection is to expand vision and awareness of who we are, so we can create wholeness in life by seeing our shadow in the mirror of our partner. Mirrors reflect the image presented. They do not create the image.

The motivation for a Leaf is to create and re-create without loss of movement. The reward is a sense of freedom. The motivation for a Trunk is accomplishment, and the reward is completion.

The keys to facilitate this bridge in a personal relationship are:

1. Accept the difference in your interpretations of reality.

2. Accept your Point of Power and your natural rhythm.

3. Recognize and claim your value in life.

4. Be willing to expand your reality by seeing and feeling life from a different point of view.

5. Learn how to communicate your reality to your partner, and how to hear your partner's communication. The Leaf must give more details, information and guidelines, not because you are wrong or being pinned down, but so your partner has some idea what you are talking about. Your partner doesn't live in your head! As a Trunk, you need to request information and ask questions necessary to fill in your missing data. Your partner is not being secretive or withholding information intentionally. They don't know you need more information. They are not your resident psychic.

6. Release your expectations that your partner is going to change and see life as you do. The more you each claim your Point of Power, the more you can use acceptance and love as the building blocks of this bridge, and let each other have your own view of life and not make each other wrong for this.

7. Allow your partner's reality to expand your vision and participation in life.

8. If you are a Leaf, learn to make clear commitments: dinner, meetings, appointments, etc. A clear commitment does not impede you or imprison you; you can always reschedule. Clear commitments allow your creativity to have a clear path to travel on. If you are a Trunk, learn to allow commitments to change and do not take this as a rejection of you. Change can always be used as an unexpected gift for you to discover new ways to respond.

    Life is continually changing, and Leaves resist making social commitments for fear something better might happen and they will miss an opportunity. The Trunks expect commitments to be kept. This is a major place of stretch for Leaves and Trunks to bring this into balance. To choose again must be an option for Leaves, or they feel trapped. To be able to rely on the commitment is part of the safety and balance of a Trunk's life, otherwise they will lose trust and feel rejected.

9. Be willing to hear your heart first. Live your love, and have the courage to tell the truth and recommit to the relationship daily. No vows or commitment can be alive without daily attention.

10. Don't take everything personally.

11. Have fun. You are on the same team. Return all conflict to a place of love, forgiveness and acceptance, daily.

Each of us must take responsibility for our true feelings, and act them out in our lives. Communicate with your partner and be willing to create options until you find a process for your ideas and love to be shared in the relationship.

Many of the couples I have spent time with, work with this combination of Points of Power. Even though they hear this information and learn the ideas, it is a whole different story to apply this in your life, when you are right in the middle of a conflict or upset. The more trust you have developed in your relationship, of yourself and each other, the easier it is to bring in new concepts for you both to relate to in a new way. If trust is present, this can really be an exciting adventure together, and add new life to the relationship.

Be careful not to use this information as an excuse not to listen, learn or cooperate with each other, just because you are a Leaf or a Trunk. No Point of Power, or combination of them, predetermines willingness and cooperation.

One couple I worked with for about two years learned about Point of Power and felt hopeful they could make changes. They were really at odds and considering separation. When we introduced this information and they became aware that they were a Leaf/Trunk combination, this provided a whole new approach for them to use in discovering each other and change how they were relating. They really worked with these ideas and went through a lot of struggles. Every so often we'd meet and fine-tune the process and boost their possibility thinking so they could continue.

They made a great deal of progress over the two years, and ended up divorcing anyway. Each of them was clearer and stronger in their own identity when they separated. As they claimed their individuality, they discovered more freedom of their individual creativity, and decided living separately would support them the most, at this time. They were able to develop a very loving supportive friendship that is still on-going.

When you discover who you really are, sometimes it changes the way you see and relate to your partner. The end result can be a clearer relationship filled with more love and respect for each other, no matter how the relationship is set up.

BUSINESS RELATIONSHIPS

Most businesses employ more Branches and Trunks than Leaves, because most businesses are creating products or supporting social systems for the public. Leaves initiate movement in business with ideas, and their ideas affect many lives in one company, so we really don't need as many Leaves as we do Branches or Trunks in most businesses. A relationship between a Leaf and Trunk in business is often filled with a lot of judgment.

For example, a scenario may be:

"I hired Sue as my assistant because I needed to be supported. She's so slow, I could finish these tasks faster than she does and save money too," Joan, a Leaf, complains.

Sue, a Trunk Point of Power says, "This woman is so unreasonable! Nothing ever satisfies her. No matter how fast I work or what I do, she always wants more and is so unappreciative of what I do. If she'd stop changing her mind every five minutes, maybe I could get something done, besides listen to her."

Needless to say, they are not talking to each other, just complaining to others about their distress with each other. This adds to their stress and breakdown in communication. Without understanding each other's Point of Power, or having a Branch translator, this relationship will be based on misunderstandings, judgments, criticism, frustration and lack of appreciation for each other, because there is such a gap in their realities. Once this negative feedback circle gets started in a relationship, it takes sincere commitment, from both parties, to change these attitudes of blame to appreciation and respect.

If the employer is a Leaf and is directly working with a Trunk person in a position that requires consistency in details, rarely will the employer value the efficiency of this employee because in their reality, "Nothing is ever done on time or fast enough," because the visionary consciousness *already sees it complete*. Why is it taking so long?

A Trunk employee is motivated by being given a task and completing it and being acknowledged for the completed task. If the main response from the employer is criticism because "it took too long," and there is no acknowledgment for the efficiency of the project, resentment begins to build in the relationship. This pattern between employer and employee will dramatically affect the efficiency, productivity and morale of a department or company.

For the highest efficiency and creativity level in a business, it is important to assess the position to be filled; what Point of Power is required to fill the position and how the people involved will work together. A communication bridge must always be built between a Leaf and a Trunk position, followed by respect for the uniqueness of each other, in order for there to be a harmonious and productive work environment.

Business relationships can be more explosive than personal relationships, because they're created on expectation, based on job performance—from an impersonal view—and easily generate blame and resentment if the expectations are not met.

The keys to creating a workable bridge for this business relationship are:

1. Accept the differences in your view of life.

2. Realize there are many ways to accomplish something in life.

3. Explore the options provided by each other's reality.

4. Know that you can maintain your reality, even if you accept some aspects of another's reality.

5. Create a common goal based on the needs of the project. Work towards this goal together.

6. Assess your Point of Power, and make your contribution to the goal from that awareness.

7. Let go of your pictures of how the other person must respond to you, in order for you to feel acknowledged and valuable.

8. Be willing to explore the unlimited possibilities available through the varied realities in your company.

9. If you're a Leaf, you must allow time for your idea to be translated into form. This will not match your conceptual time frame and expectation of completion.

10. Leaves, use a Branch as your partner to translate and share your ideas with the Trunk. Their rhythms are compatible and allow information to be shared more easily. If you don't have access to a Branch translator, you must slow down your conceptual pace and be willing to communicate your ideas one step at a time. Be willing and patient to answer questions until the ideas are clearly understood by both of you. This will eliminate a lot of confusion and resentment later.

11. Do not judge others as inefficient if their performances don't match your conceptual pace as a Leaf. This is a key area to keep free of resentment and blame. Learn patience with yourself, so you can share it with others.

12. As a Trunk, you must ask questions and obtain the information you need to proceed with your work.

13. Release the judgment that you're never appreciated by the Leaf, by realizing their rhythm is different than yours and so are their expectations. Don't take everything so personally.

14. Accept yourself and your value in the company and on the project.

15. Be willing to hear a Leaf communicate without making yourself responsible for all the ideas you hear. Your

naturalness is to hear the idea/request and "fill it," to create a finished product. Be clear on which ideas the Leaf is asking you to follow through with and when that is to be accomplished. Then you begin. If you feel responsible to respond to all the ideas of a Leaf, without a clear assignment or plan, you will always be frustrated and feel unfulfilled in your work relationship. This is a seedbed where resentment and blame can grow.

16. If communication between a Leaf and Trunk begins to stand still or go in circles, you need to (a) stop communicating, (b) agree to a time out, (c) commit to another time to resume the conversation. If you take a break, you can usually shift the perceptions you are holding and try another avenue of communication when you meet again. Power struggles are a lose/lose.

17. Be conscious of your position in the company, and the Point of Power needed to fill it. Are you the right Point of Power for the job? The right person in the wrong position is a set up for sabotage on all levels, for everyone.

The following is a conversation and situation I worked with in consulting a company on staff relationships. This may sound familiar to you.

Newell (Leaf) is talking with Janice (Trunk) about an accounting transaction.

"Newell, the figures you need to file the report are here on page two," Janice says, pointing to them. "And on page four are the in-depth descriptions to support these totals."

"Janice, I don't want all that information and to have to sort it out. I just want the amounts that go in this report."

"Well, Newell, this is the information that will provide those totals."

"Janice, I want you to use these details and fill in pages three and four on this report for me. I need it by 4:30 today, when Jack comes for our meeting."

Very frustrated, Janice responds, "Newell, I asked you about this last Friday, and you said, 'Oh, no, it won't take me long,' and now you want me to complete this—on your time schedule. There's a good hour and a half involved in this, and I have an appointment with the C.P.A. in thirty minutes."

"Well, just reschedule the C.P.A. I need this today."

"I understand that, Newell. What you don't seem to understand is that I need to meet with the C.P.A. today, to clear up the details for our month-end report that is due tomorrow. This is the only day Tom had open this week."

"Janice, if you just get this done today before Jack comes, you can hire a 'temp' to help you close out the reports tomorrow. I really have to have this today."

Does some version of this seem familiar to you? This is a very clear example of the two different rhythms, of the Leaf and Trunk, and how life can get complicated as a result of the difference in timing. Janice could take this personally and feel unappreciated and unacknowledged or recognize the different rhythms and know there are more building blocks of cooperation needed to maintain this relationship. Newell can use this experience as an opportunity to see how this could have been planned better to make it easier for both of them, by exploring his part in the planning and how it could be different, so all the commitments can be met easily on time.

Changes like this require small daily steps of conscious co-operation in order to have the whole picture be brighter and easier for everyone. It really does take commitment on everyone's part and sometimes there are breakdowns in the best laid plans. If you have a communication plan and can explore the breakdown together, everything has an answer and a possibility of resolution and mutual satisfaction if you just keep moving with the situation and each other. The satisfaction and sense of accomplishment from persistence and perseverance are great rewards.

PARENT/CHILD RELATIONSHIPS

This type of relationship between a Leaf and a Trunk tends to be highly charged because of intense emotional patterns in families. Since our home and family is supposed to be our safe and nurturing place, we tend to experience and express our greatest fears and vulnerabilities with those we love, or want to love, the most. Our fears and vulnerable places usually do not produce our "favorite" behaviors. In families, we can see and express behaviors with each other that we rarely see displayed outside our homes. Our emotions are closer to the surface, and we react easily and unpredictably, many times, with each other. As we learn to feel safe, trust each other, and be loving and loved, our behaviors with each other can be much kinder, considerate and respectful of each member in the family.

Conflict cannot exist without a perceived enemy. It takes two parts to engage in conflict, inside of us or outside of us. The key accusation or feeling, spoken or unspoken, in most families is, you don't love me. If we feel unloved or unsafe, we tend to target the person or situation as the enemy, and begin our tactics of defense or attack. Once this begins, it is like a snowball rolling down a mountain, it gets very big, very fast, and it feels out of control and threatening to everyone involved. Thus our defenses increase, and the war is on.

As a parent figure in many young peoples' lives over the years, I have discovered every time I enrolled myself in a power struggle with the youth, I always lost, sooner or later. I also discovered, if I enrolled myself as a person, in respect of another person, regardless of their size or age, there was resolution that would work for both of us, especially if it was created by both of us, or with respect for the needs we both have.

Another great gift for me was accepting that I don't know everything and I don't have to. I can still be a good, kind, and loving parent and my children can acquire healthy answers and support in life from other people and situations, and so can I. Being a parent is one of life's most precious gifts and greatest challenges, and we have little to no training. We practice on each other, generation after generation, and the price in terms of pain and dysfunction is very high. We must stop this runaway snowball of inheritance from our ancestors and renew our commitment to love, respect and forgiveness so we can once again experience home and family as a safe and loving place.

Distress in your family can feel overwhelming and isolating, like you are the only one, and it's your fault. I want to assure you from years in this field, this is not true. As the media and life are representing, we are in this one together—rich, poor, young, old, white, black, educated, uneducated, male, female—it doesn't matter. We must go back to the drawing board on this one. The way we are doing family is in need of remodeling.

By consciously participating in each other's life, from a place of love and respect, we can restructure anything in life and renew the sacredness of family and community.

Most of our schools were set up to support Trunk and Branch learning styles, so the Leaves and Roots many times get labeled hyperactive, attention deficit, or mentally or emotionally retarded. The systems and methods of a Trunk and those of society as a whole, do not "hear" or support the needs and naturalness of a Leaf child.

If you are a Leaf Point of Power, parenting a Trunk child, you may experience expectations and judgments. "This child is so slow in everything s/he does they never gets things done." Coming from a Leaf perspective (formless), this may seem true, especially when you want something accomplished in form, and you expect it to materialize as quickly as you visualized it. This is not possible, and your Trunk child may be creating and responding as quickly as s/he can to accomplish your request and gain your approval.

If you are a Trunk parenting a Leaf child, your criticism or concern could be, "This child never listens to me. I asked him or her to do this and s/he said yes, and now s/he acts like s/he never even heard me ask him or her." This is a common point of stress in this combination. Leaf children are constantly creating and re-creating in their visionary minds. They hear you in the moment (most of the time), and they may have the best of intentions, and actually leave you to go do the task, and on their way, think of something else or see something new, and their mind follows what comes up in the moment. Chances are, they will not remember to return to your request. So many magical things have come up in their mind since you last talked that their mind is headed in a different direction now.

A helpful way to support your request being heard and remembered is to ask Leaf children to look at you (be on their eye level), touch their arm and say to them, "Listen to me, this is what I want you to do." When you have made your request (still touching their arm), ask them to tell you what they heard you say. If their response is unclear, repeat this procedure again, and help them clarify your request in their words. When they get it, touch their head, and acknowledge them. Cheer them on. We are all inspired by praise. Your visionary child may stay focused in their conscious/linear mind more easily when you look them in the eye and have physical contact with them as you communicate. It helps to anchor in your information and there is a greater possibility of their remembering what you said. Never 100%, just more often.

Without knowing these differences, and the place of innocence that is generated by both of you, you can begin to become resentful or disrespectful of each other. This erodes your basic sense of trust in your relationship and can spawn many hours and years of pain, if your naturalness is not recognized and redirected by both of you.

The keys to building a bridge of love and communication are:

1. Accept the differences in your views of reality.

2. It doesn't matter how you saw life as a child. That may not be your child's reality at all.

3. Because your child thinks, believes or behaves differently than you did, or do now, does not make either of you wrong.

4. Parenting is a learning experience for both parent and child. NO ONE EXPECTS YOU TO BE PERFECT EXCEPT YOU. Release yourself from this unrealistic expectation so you can create choice and options in your life that will work.

5. Release the need for your child to be an extension of you. You do not have to satisfy friends, neighbors and relatives. This is a partnership experience with your child and must fulfill both of you. Release your pictures of how love looks and feels and how you each must behave.

6. If you're a Leaf and are parenting a child who is a Trunk, you may think the child has learning disabilities, because they

don't do anything fast enough. That's possible, but you'll need to consider the possibility that s/he may have a Point of Power different from yours; that what's needed is acceptance, love and approval. Perhaps nothing is wrong, just different.

7. Acknowledge your child as an individual. Support him or her as an individual, no matter what size or age. As a parent you can learn from your child the innocence and truth of life.

8. If you're a Trunk parenting a Leaf child, release the judgment that you're doing something wrong to make your child behave this way. These children are not irresponsible because they don't follow through with all their ideas and projects. Their naturalness is to create and re-create, not implement. They need support to learn implementation.

9. Teach Leaf children how to focus on one thing at a time, to gather the information they need to make clear decisions in their life. This is the main support they will need to feel confident and experience accomplishment. Whatever the task, cleaning their room, brushing their teeth, doing homework, picking up toys, follow these steps:

    (a) Include the child in the creation of this process.

    (b) Create options so they feel they have choice and are a part of the process. (This is essential for all children.)

    (c) Agree on a completion time, and allow them to decide when they will do it, within that time frame.

    Implementation is not a Point of Power for a Leaf child. Our school systems are designed to reward implementation and completion in a certain way. This experience of confinement will be very frustrating for a visionary child. Their frustrated energy may be expressed through disruptive behavior at home and school. The Leaf child must have more freedom of movement, mentally and physically.

10. Continued, imposed limitations can result in behavior extremes. Either rebellious, aggressive, angry behavior; or depressed, apathetic, non-motivated behavior.

11. As a parent or a child, there is always more than one way to accomplish something. Have this be part of the joy of discovery together.

12. No one in the family is wrong because there are different realities. Make the home big enough in vision to have room for all Points of Power to have freedom of expression. Cooperation begins with acceptance.

13. Have fun practicing family together and being curious about life. Give it permission to change easily.

14. Allow your relationship to live and grow through love.

I happened to be next door when I got to watch this scene. David (Dad, who is a Trunk) and Stephen (9 years old and a Leaf child) are working together on the car. The carburetor needs an adjustment.

"Stephen, hand me the crescent wrench," Dad says, as he looks up.

Wide-eyed, Stephen asks, "The crescent wrench, which one is that, Dad?"

"Stephen, I showed you last week what a crescent wrench looks like. I didn't think you were paying attention."

"I really was, Dad. I'll find it." He mumbles to himself as he picks through the tools. Then he shouts, "Here Dad, is this it?"

"No, Stephen! Forget it, I'll have to do it myself."

"Wait, Dad, wait-let me try once more." He mumbles and fumbles through the tools some more and gleefully hollers, "Is this it?"

"That's it, Stephen. Now pay attention so you'll remember next time."

Relieved, Stephen begins to explore the engine. "Dad, this gray tube here, what is it?"

"Where, Stephen?" Dad asks with exasperation.

"This one, next to this round thing that looks like metal. Wow, Dad, look at this! What is this? I'll bet this goes really fast when the engine's on. Can we turn on the engine, and see it move?" Stephen is excited and jumping near the car.

"Stephen, use your head. Does it look like we can turn on the car while I'm doing this work? And stop bouncing all over. I thought you wanted to help me."

Stephen looks up, looks at the engine, turns and decides to explore the tool bench, beginning with more questions.

I really had to laugh at this whole scenario. It is so common. When we as parents are doing stressful tasks or really concentrating, it is sometimes difficult to appreciate the curiosity and magic of our children. Stephen was undaunted. He loved being with Dad in the garage, forbidden territory unless he was with Dad, because things came up missing and never found their way home to the tool box or workbench.

David and Jill (Stephen's mom and dad) and I have had casual conversations about the Tree of Life. They are working on applying it for their family. You can see some experiences make it a little more difficult than others to consciously appreciate each other when we are occupied with our daily routines of life. This tool is like any other. The more we use it the more skill we have with it.

Stephen is a very bright and energetic child and sometimes it takes all three of us to keep up with his ambition and curiosity. We are all learning a lot in the process. Stephen is a great teacher.

Chapter 9

How Do Branches and Roots Communicate?

PERSONAL RELATIONSHIPS

The Branches and the Roots have a relationship with form. Even though their reality is very different in expression, this common thread provides a place to begin communication. The Roots relate with life at a foundational level, very solid, stable and grounded. Being present in life is the power of this part of the Tree of Life. The Branches translate the formless into form. They experience creation through new beginnings, and don't want long-term involvement with the end result. They love starting a new business, a new project, a new hobby, a new adventure and want to continue expanding their creation, project, or relationship. They want their participation to manifest in form.

Branches are the Translators. They have great affinity with the abstract and the formless and they love creating with form. Since this is their naturalness, even though they are separated from the Roots by the Trunk, they can more easily make that transition, and share time with the Roots, and still feel a sense of their own Point of Power, and an understanding of the Roots and the world they live in.

Motivational needs are very different between these two, and without conscious communication, there is little in common. Their pace of life is different. The Branches are motivated by many ideas and change. They have very little patience with a slower pace of living. The Roots motivation is to be "in the moment," fully participating with their body, mind and emotions. To communicate with each other easily, it is necessary for each to recognize and respect the other's rhythm. Branches have a tendency to be impatient with the Roots' slower rhythm, and the Roots can feel pushed by the Branches.

Their rewards are different, too. Branches want to quickly create and go to another project, or expand the present one or bring something new into their life. The Roots want to find something that works and stick with it.

If this relationship between a Branch and a Root were to be a long-term, daily experience, they would definitely need to create guidelines for their communication to flow easily and to satisfy the needs they each have for their natural rhythm. By staying focused on their mutual relationship with form, Branches and Roots working together are a very powerful team. This relationship combination may present what seems to be opposite viewpoints of reality, from which they may be able to experience a more balanced way to live. With commitment and willingness from both people, it is really quite workable and most of the time easily maintained. It does require conscious recognition of the needs of each other and clarification of the desired results. This is a valuable connection for both and can be quite refreshing to share in each other's world.

Extremes are not balance. They provide guidelines from which we can create balance. Balance is a key to our wellness. Since this is an experience most of us are seeking, we seem to begin our search for balance from the extremes in our life where we do not know what we want. Through some of the distortions we experienced as we grew up, we began to create some reactionary patterns to our environment, usually displaying resistance or resentment to people or situations. We learned to motivate ourself from these reactionary patterns and behaviors. This is negative motivation, or reactive behavior.

Most of us are clearer on what we don't want than what we do want, so this is a good place to start our discovery of what we do want. Every time you hear yourself say (or think) "I don't want this or that," ask yourself, "What *do* I want?"

When I discovered this pattern of motivation in my life, I spent a year exploring all the places that were started from a negative motivation and I really understood why my life had felt like such a struggle. It takes a lot of energy to accomplish what I truly want, if my starting point is a negative motivation. I would constantly have to clear out the things in my life that got created through my confusion.

Once you begin to examine life through your "I don't wants," you can consciously begin to make choices on what you do want. Thus the pendulum swing of life can be negotiated and directed to a place of balance by choosing for your life rather than reacting to your life. Once you begin to bridge your own reality consciously, it is a lot easier to bridge with another's reality.

This reminds me of a conversation between Sally (Roots) and Lenny (Branches). They had been talking for quite a while about needing to get away. Their relationship always seemed to have a point of tension in it, and they felt frustrated most of the time. They thought if they took a vacation together it might help them. Unfortunately, this new adventure actually accelerated their confusion and frustration with each other, because their Points of Power are so different.

One point of tension in the relationship was the pace at which they both liked to move, Sally, very slowly and methodically, and Lenny, quickly and spontaneously. When they started to plan this trip, you can imagine how their frustration increased. Lenny, of course, was bringing home all kinds of brochures, magazines, articles and suggestions. Sally was still considering if she really wanted to go away. "Maybe a week at home would be just as good." Since Lenny was ready to go, he didn't even want to relate to Sally's indecision, so he was into marketing the plan and getting on with the trip.

By the time they came to see me, they were not sure they even wanted to be in the relationship, let alone take a trip with each other. We talked about the Tree of Life and their Point of Power as Branches and Roots. After quite a bit of conversation and exploration of this idea, they began to see the pattern in all their relationship, more than just this trip. I gave Sally and Lenny these keys for bridging these differences, and they practiced them for a couple of weeks and called me to let me know they were going to Bali for a month.

The keys to help facilitate this bridge are:

1. Accept the differences.

2. Give yourself and your partner permission to be who you are.

3. Find the common goals and visions for your relationship. What do you both enjoy? What goals and values do you have? Build on these common points of interest. Be in continuous communication about your lives. You must consciously maintain communication through sharing, or there will be no bridge for conversation, creation, or commitment.

4. Give yourselves permission to have fun and laugh with each other as you share and grow together. Humor is the best glue to hold a bridge together. It lightens the pressures on both of you.

5. Keep practicing, together and apart.

BUSINESS RELATIONSHIPS

The same principles apply to business and personal relationships regarding motivation and reward. The dynamics of the relationship may be altered because there's usually less personal involvement.

The keys to help facilitate the employment bridge are:

1. Accept the differences.

2. Determine if the right person (Point of Power) is in the right job position. If the job and the person match in their Point of Power, everything about the work will be easier, more efficient and productive, inspiring and creative. If the job and the person do not match in their Point of Power, no matter what changes and adjustments are made, "something" will always feel like it isn't working. This reduces the efficiency and productivity and the work will always feel like a

challenge or struggle. When a person and position do not match in their Point of Power, the person will subconsciously be sabotaging their job until they release themselves to a position that matches their Point of Power.

3. Stay commited to your Point of Power and support the other person's freedom to express their Point of Power.

4. Have fun. It's only a job!

As a consultant, I witnessed the following conversation in a business meeting I was attending. This conversation took place between two men who had not had one work-related conversation that worked for them in two years until we did a Point of Power Training for them. This conversation was three months after the training.

Sam (Branch) and Charlie (Roots) are in conversation about the company's next project. Charlie has been a member of the assembly department for twelve years in the Sound Systems Production Company.

Sam hands a paper to Charlie, and says, "Charlie, this blueprint will show you the five changes that we need to produce in our V12 Model speaker to upgrade the whole sound system in Project Ten." Charlie studies the paper. Sam watches, knowing how thorough Charlie is.

Sam asks, "What do you think, Charlie?"

"Well, I need to study this a little, Sam. Can I tell you tomorrow or Wednesday morning?"

"Sure, Charlie," Sam replies. "Would you review it for me with these two questions in mind: Number one, is this going to dramatically improve the quality of sound in Model V12, in your opinion? And number two, do you want to be involved with the new project?"

Charlie looks up, silent, stands up, blueprint in hand, turns and, on his way out, says, "O.K., Sam, talk to you tomorrow."

Sam knows he's been heard, and if Charlie has any questions, they'll come up after he studies the blueprint and gets a "feel" for the changes.

Sam and Charlie made a commitment to change the way they were relating to each other, in order to accomplish their desire to work together, and not be in conflict all the time. This conversation indicates how carefully they are proceeding, because it is not really natural for them yet. They are breaking old ways of reacting to each other. They both commented on how much more they enjoy their work now.

PARENT/CHILD RELATIONSHIPS

Again, the principles are the same. The dynamics are different because there's a great deal of emotional involvement. In all relationships we are either part of the problem or part of the solution. Sometimes it is more difficult to see our part as a parent, because we are so intimately involved with our children. As a rule, our children also "push our buttons," on our own level of vulnerability and woundedness, and many times we are reacting to our children from our own confusion and pain and projecting this on them.

Then, on top of this, if we add a difference in our view of life and our Point of Power, the problem can be very confusing and the emotions highly charged.

The keys to reduce this frustration and increase the parent/child bridge are given from the parent's point of view. If a child is old enough to participate in the communication, the reverse is also applicable. The keys are:

1. Accept the differences.

2. Release judgment on yourself. Be real and truthful about your own vulnerability, so you can honestly be present with your child's feelings and needs.

3. Release the expectation that you should be a perfect parent and know everything. You're still practicing with life and learning daily.

4. Recognize the child as a powerful partner in this relationship. Respect the child as a person, no matter what age or size.

5. Acknowledge the child as an individual, and let them develop their own ideas and personality.

6. Accept your moments of resentment for the huge responsibility of being a parent, and feeling so untrained and unqualified for the task.

Acceptance, love and re-commitment to each other surpasses any fears either of you may have. You are both doing the best you know how to do, for the moment you are in and the training and experience you have. The most important thing is to stay on the same team, even through conflict. Do not allow yourselves to become enemies in your own home. No one wins in this power struggle if you are not on the same team. There can be no power struggle without two parties involved. Recommit to love and being on the same team to break the power struggle. Something always changes when you do this.

The following is a situation that demonstrates staying on the same team (Mom is a Branch, and Johnny is a seven-year-old Roots person).

Mom comes into Johnny's room, excitedly pulling new purchases out of bags, and exclaiming, "Look, Johnny, I found these adorable curtains with great spaceships on them, and a new bedspread to match!" Johnny looks up, appearing uninterested and says nothing.

Mom comes closer and holds up a curtain, asking, "What do you think, Johnny?"

"They're ugly!" he says.

"Ugly? How can you say that? These are the latest thing, Johnny. I thought you liked spaceships."

"I do, Mom, to read about them. I like the curtains and bedspread I have," he says as he plops down on the bed.

"I know, Honey, but they're so old and fading. I thought . . ."

"I like these, Mom," Johnny says defensively.

Mom sits down beside him, feeling disappointed, and asks, "What do you like about the old ones, Johnny?"

"I like the animals and trees."

Mom sighs as she stands, picks up the new curtains and, as she's folding them, says, "How about this? I'll leave these folded here in your room, and you check them out in the next couple days. Okay? See what you think. If you don't want them, maybe we can talk about shopping together for new ones."

"Okay, Mom." Johnny returns to the game he was playing when Mom came in.

It has taken me years to incorporate these ideas and practices with my children and grandchildren. It is worth every moment of re-training it took because it has enriched our family life so much and allowed a lot of our past behavior to change. We have new ways to relate to each other that give us many more loving options than we had before.

Chapter 10

Can Leaves and Roots Have a Conversation?

The Leaves and the Roots have a major gap in their realities. When you look at the Tree of Life, you see the Branches and the Trunk are missing or at least not present in this combination. With these frequencies not consciously present, these two Points of Power *really* have to stretch to communicate and understand each other. For short-term experiences, they can be like a breath of fresh air for each other. For any longer relationship some conscious understanding of each other's Point of Power is necessary, otherwise the Leaves and the Roots have a tendency to be judgmental or projecting on each other since their realities are so very different. It is difficult to understand how each other functions without a translator of some kind. The translator can be acceptance of each other, another person acting as a liaison between the Leaves and the Roots, or the conscious awareness of each person and their Point of Power and how they believe. Understanding there are other realities, equally as valid as yours with a different focus in life, reduces the stress.

The Leaves can find the Roots very real, very grounding. You can always find these people! They are consistent, an attribute that supports the Leaves, especially if they do not have to be the one being consistent. They really do appreciate a certain amount of this support in their lives. Many times the Leaves will participate in activities that appear to be the natural rhythm of the Roots. When they do this, they use the frequency of the Roots, energy in themselves to ground and stabilize their reality, which is always moving and changing. In this way, the Leaves use this foundational energy as a point of balance for themselves. This may be done through gardening, pottery, painting, mechanical projects or massage—anything that involves the body and allows the hands to create.

The Roots can experience all kinds of possibilities they hadn't considered before being around the ever changing and moving mind of the Leaves. Since the mind of the Leaves creates in a unique way, the Roots appreciate this experience. Observing this creativity is usually enough. Being with the Leaves provides an opportunity for the Roots to have a new vantage point of life. It may not necessarily be an experience they would want in their own life, and it does give them a chance to have movement and action come into their life in a different way. The Leaves' participation with the Roots is like double-digging the earth; we spade the earth to introduce air and prepare the soil so new life can emerge. Being with the Leaves definitely stirs things up for the Roots. Some of the ways Roots can embrace the gifts of the Leaves are through being exposed to new projects, participating in new adventures together and exploring life together. Since Roots are not interested in philosophizing, the time spent together is an experience rather than a discussion.

The relationship between the Leaves and Roots is like a good movie in life, something you choose to do for a specific purpose, appreciate it, learn from it, and then return to your own reality. Those in a relationship in this combination have such different views of life that they are rarely in unison. If they spend time together it is short-term for a desired goal, and then they may not see each other for awhile or not again. These relationships occur most frequently in business situations or personal relationships that come together intermittently.

I had the opportunity to be present when this conversation took place:

James (Leaf) and Bill (Roots) were walking through James's yard, just admiring the beauty. Bill had been involved as the gardener and designer of this wonderful yard for seven years. Bill looked at James and smiled and said, "Bill, I saw a beautiful begonia I love and I want to plant it here. The color would be so nice in this corner."

"Begonias are nice, James, but they like to live in shady spots. I'm concerned this would be too hot for them."

"Oh, really? Well, that's okay."

Bill and James continue to walk through the garden, admiring the many plants, trees and flowers. "Bill, what was the name of that plant Jane talked about? It had dark, large leaves and I think it had pink blossoms. No, maybe it was white, well, anyway, I can't remember. Do you know what kind of plant I'm talking about? Would that be okay in that corner?"

"I'm not sure what plant you are talking about, James. It sounds pretty. Could you get more information for me and then I can let you know if it will work there?"

"Okay, Bill, I'll check it out," James says, as he glances around the yard.

"Bill, look at this bush. This is a great bush. Is this new?"

"No, James, that's two years old."

"How come I never noticed it before?"

"You did. You picked it out, and I planted it for you."

"Oh, well," James smiles sheepishly. "It's grown a lot, hasn't it?"

They both laugh and do a high five.

I've know James and Bill for about five years and these kind of interactions have happened frequently over the years. When I first met them and heard these kind of interactions, they were not pleasant. They usually ended in one or both of them being angry and accusing the other of not listening. Bill usually felt discounted by James, because he never remembered what Bill had done or which plants he had brought in to the garden, at James request. Since, James was creating a new "vision" every time he walked in the garden, he always wanted to change the plan, as he was seeing it today, forgetting the plan they had worked out two weeks ago. This frustrated and discouraged Bill, because he felt like James never appreciated anything he ever did, because he always wanted to change it.

We talked about Point of Power, over the years, and they learned to recognize their own natural rhythms and how different they each were. This is reflected in their work also. James is a corporate pilot, on call all the time, and sometimes away from home a week or two at a time. Bill lives at James's house in his own cottage, and is the caretaker of the land and animals, as well as the gardener, while James is away.

Their working and personal relationship has blossomed considerably over the years and they have both become more accepting and respectful of each other. They don't spend a lot of time together, and when they do now they really can have a pleasant time together and are discovering more things they have in common, as they talk with each other, even though they are very different people in many ways.

Epilogue

In the last few years that I have been experiencing Point of Power, I can truly see the changes in my own life. What a valuable reference point this has become for me. I hope you have fun playing with this information in your life, with your family and friends.

Joan Follendore, my wonderful editor and agent, shared this information with me and I wanted to pass it on to you. These are excerpts from "The Music of God," by Rev. John Williams Jones, in 1916.

> Nature is more full of music than we imagine. It has remained for modern science to develop this truth with startling vividness. All music is motion, and underlying all motion is the law of vibration. That which we call matter trembles—and its tremors go forth in waves of vibrations which have been estimated with scientific precision that staggers our imagination and stimulates our faith.
>
> Light really sings. The sunshine is music. . . . Thus is all nature like a great orchestra giving forth vibrations in different notes and chords or color. There is a melody and harmony of life in all its forms.
>
> All this vast universe of matter, pulsing with the power of hidden electricity, vibrating with the force of unseen heat, radiating with the glow of immeasurable light and breaking forth here and there with the glory of grand, beauteous color, all the universe is a voice and a song, so that the "Music of the spheres" is indeed and truly "music of God."

You are a Divine instrument of sound and light and the relationship between your physical, mental and emotional bodies creates a rhythm that is uniquely yours, designed to allow the voice of the Soul to have expression in your life. In order for you to dance with this rhythm consciously, you too must come to a place of willingness to recognize and accept all that you are.

You are an expression of "Love in Action" in this human form. As you allow your belief system to embrace your Divine Essence and become a conscious partner in all the realities you live in, your life becomes the Great Adventure your Soul designed it to be. Joy is the reward for an intimate relationship with your Soul.

For more information on personal or group sessions, seminars, trainings, corporate consultations, or teacher/trainer certification you may contact:

Point of Power Center
Box 60
Kapaa, Kauai, Hawaii 96746
(808) 823-0314

Glossary

Caretaker: anyone who assumes responsibility for another's behavior or welfare, when that individual is capable of being responsible for themselves.

Creativity: a living expression of our Soul, delivered in our life through our naturalness, the Divine Child within.

Denial: recognized behaviors or beliefs we refuse to accept, acknowledge, appreciate, re-evaluate, eliminate or restructure in our lives, in order to create more wholeness.

Distortions: our view of Life affected by our fears, beliefs, behaviors and experiences, based on partial truths and illusions.

Gift: an experience, situation or person, presented in our life that offers us the opportunity to grow.

Judgment: derived from a foundation of right and wrong; prejudged and conditioned beliefs, based on a learned value of ourselves, others and life.

Naturalness: the unadulterated, creative part of our Being, free from outer distortions and influences of life.

Point of Power: the place in us where the Divine Child of our Soul is free to speak, sing our song of life, create, play, love and be loved naturally and purely, without limitations or distortions.

Present: allowing ourselves to show up in life with and for us; a virgin experience—in the now; being maximally conscious/participating in the moment.

Process: a method of response to the issues and changes in life; what we have learned to do in order to create movement in our lives in a way that works for us.

Reality: our perception of the world we live in, colored by our Point of Power, our beliefs, behaviors and interaction with life.

Release: letting go of illusions of yourself and your reality; allowing movement in your life—mentally, physically, emotionally and spiritually; letting go of mental controls so illusions can come forward and be identified, constructively redirecting the power from the illusions.

Remember: the act of going beyond our beliefs, fears and distortions. Recognizing and accepting our Point of Power—the Divine Child within, joy, our Eternal Selves.

Three-Dimensional Reality: experience of Life based almost entirely on sensory feedback from and through the body senses and the linear mind.

Translator: someone who can hear an idea or concept, and transform it into action, systems, words; between two Points of Power.

Wholeness: an integrated balance of mental, physical, spiritual and emotional bodies.